MAX
notes®

Charlotte Brontë's

Jane Eyre

LONDON PUBLIC LIBRARY

Text by
Barbara Quintero
(M.A. New York University)
Department of English
Marymount Manhattan College
New York, New York

Illustrations by
Karen Pica

Research & Education Association

MAXnotes® for
JANE EYRE

Copyright © 2005, 1996 by Research & Education
Association, Inc. All rights reserved. No part of
this book may be reproduced in any form without
permission of the publisher.

Printed in the United States of America

Library of Congress Control Number 2005901276

International Standard Book Number 0-87891-022-0

MAXnotes® and REA® are registered trademarks of Research &
Education Association, Inc., Piscataway, New Jersey 08854

B05

What **MAXnotes**® *Will Do for You*

This book is intended to help you absorb the essential contents and features of Charlotte Brontë's *Jane Eyre* and to help you gain a thorough understanding of the work. The book has been designed to do this more quickly and effectively than any other study guide.

For best results, this **MAXnotes** book should be used as a companion to the actual work, not instead of it. The interaction between the two will greatly benefit you.

To help you in your studies, this book presents the most up-to-date interpretations of every section of the actual work, followed by questions and fully explained answers that will enable you to analyze the material critically. The questions also will help you to test your understanding of the work and will prepare you for discussions and exams.

Meaningful illustrations are included to further enhance your understanding and enjoyment of the literary work. The illustrations are designed to place you into the mood and spirit of the work's settings.

The **MAXnotes** also include summaries, character lists, explanations of plot, and chapter-by-chapter analyses. A biography of the author and discussion of the work's historical context will help you put this literary piece into the proper perspective of what is taking place.

The use of this study guide will save you the hours of preparation time that would ordinarily be required to arrive at a complete grasp of this work of literature. You will be well prepared for classroom discussions, homework, and exams. The guidelines that are included for writing papers and reports on various topics will prepare you for any added work which may be assigned.

The **MAXnotes** will take your grades "to the max."

Larry B. Kling
Chief Editor

Contents

> **Each Chapter includes List of Characters,
> Summary, Analysis, Study Questions and
> Answers, and Suggested Essay Topics.**

MAXnotes® are simply the best - but don't just take our word for it...

"... I have told every bookstore in the area to carry your MAXnotes. They are the only notes I recommend to my students. There is no comparison between MAXnotes and all other notes ..."
   – High School Teacher & Reading Specialist,
   Arlington High School, Arlington, MA

"... The two MAXnotes titles that I have used have been very, very useful in helping me understand the subject matter reviewed. Thank you for creating the MAXnotes series ..."
   – Student, Morrisville, PA

A Glance at Some of the Characters

Jane Eyre

Edward Rochester

Mr. Brocklehurst

Adele Varens

Helen Burns

St. John Rivers

Mrs. Sarah Reed

Introduction

The Life and Work of Charlotte Brontë

Charlotte Brontë, born on April 21, 1816, was the third child of Maria Branwell Brontë and the Reverend Patrick Brontë. Originally of Irish descent, the Brontës moved to Haworth, a village on the Yorkshire moors, when Patrick Brontë was appointed rector of the Haworth parish church. The Haworth Parsonage, set high on a hill, overlooked the church graveyard on one side and the wild desolate moors of Yorkshire on the other.

It was in this environment that the six Brontë children, Maria, Elizabeth, Charlotte, Branwell (the only son), Emily, and Anne formed their own imaginary world, creating stories and poems inspired by a box of toy soldiers. The written word was valued in the Brontë household as the Reverend aspired to literary success, and the small library in his study was readily available to the children.

Tragedy struck the family early and persistently. Soon after the move to Haworth, Maria Branwell Brontë, exhausted from bearing six children in seven years, died of cancer after a long illness. Charlotte was only five years old.

The Reverend made several unsuccessful attempts to remarry, and eventually called his sister-in-law Elizabeth to Haworth to help raise the children.

In 1824, Maria, eleven years old, and Elizabeth, ten, were sent to a new school for the daughters of clergymen at Cowan Bridge. Charlotte, eight, and Emily, six, joined them that same year. Due to the unsanitary and harsh conditions of the school, a typhoid epidemic occurred. Maria and Elizabeth both died of tuberculosis. Charlotte and Emily were brought home immediately.

In 1831, Charlotte was again sent away to be educated–at Roe Head, an exclusive school fifteen miles from Haworth. After less than a year, she returned home to teach her sisters, then, in 1835, returned to Roe Head as a teacher, only to be called home again when Aunt Elizabeth died. For a brief time she worked as a governess, then returned home to Haworth, and for the next few years tutored her sisters, Emily and Anne, while continuing to write.

At the age of twenty–six, Charlotte, hoping to open her own school in Haworth, enrolled in a small private school in Brussels to study foreign languages. There she formed a one–sided romantic attachment to the married headmaster, Constantin Heger, and continued to write him letters after returning to England.

In 1846, after discovering that Emily and Anne had been writing poetry, Charlotte convinced her sisters to self–publish a book of their poems. Under the pseudonyms Currer (Charlotte), Ellis (Emily), and Acton (Anne) Bell, they published their first book of poems. Only two copies sold, but that did not deter them from each writing a novel. Charlotte's *Jane Eyre* was published in 1847, followed by Anne's *Agnes Gray,* and Emily's *Wuthering Heights.*

Success came immediately to Charlotte, and she continued to write throughout her life. *Shirley* was published in 1849, *Villette* was published in 1853, and *The Professor* was published after her death, in 1857.

Unfortunately, Charlotte's siblings Emily, Anne, and Branwell were all dead by 1849, and Charlotte was left alone at Haworth to care for her father. In 1852, Charlotte accepted a marriage proposal from her father's curate, Arthur Bell Nichols, and continued to live at Haworth. In 1855, pregnant with her first child, Charlotte caught a chill while walking on the moors, and died on March 31, at the age of thirty-nine.

Historical Background

The Victorian Age refers to the period in England when Queen Victoria reigned, (1837–1901). During this time, the Industrial Revolution created profound economical changes in society. The introduction of machinery changed England from primarily an agricultural country to an industrial one, and created a great social upheaval. Production lead to the rise of factories in the cities, and the need for factory workers. Farm workers migrated from rural to urban communities in large numbers, which created mass unemployment. The living conditions for the masses were poor; children and women were employed in factories and paid extremely low wages.

New class distinctions emerged from this growth of industrial production. The "gentry" were the landowners, the unemployed were the "poor," and a new "middle class" emerged. The representative middle class man included the shop-keeper, the merchant, and the village parson.

The Victorian middle class adhered to the social conventions of family domesticity and religion. Charlotte Brontë's time was characterized by public moralizing, a stifling religious outlook, and private hypocrisy. Victorian gentlemen publicly preached morality but patroned brothels. In Victorian society, propriety and prudence were the accepted virtues.

The idealized Victorian family of the middle class was a fraction of the population, which included many people living in factory slums. There were great gaps between the rich and the poor, and many orphaned children were exposed to extreme suffering. All of this existed outside official notice of Victorian worship of family life, domesticity, and the hearth.

Middle class women were expected to marry, produce large families, and tend to their children. Unmarried middle class women were limited to respectable work as a governess or teacher. Women who were poor worked in the factories.

Women's restrictions were evident in the very garments that they wore, and they were expected to act with the utmost propriety. An excerpt from *The Habits of Good Society*, published anonymously in 1855, describes the proper behavior for women upon entering a room:

> Her face should wear a smile; she should not rush in headforemost; a graceful bearing, a light step, an elegant bend to common acquaintance, a cordial pressure, not shaking, of the hand extended to her, are requisite of a lady. Let her sink gently into a chair.... Her feet should scarcely be shown and not crossed....

Obedience in children was expected and cherished as proper behavior. Punishments might be beatings or solitary confinement. The method of imposing self-discipline or severe punishment in this world, and a threat of terrible penalties in the world to come (the Ten Commandments were often quoted), kept many children in line. Children were either educated at home by a governess or sent away to school where the treatment was often cruel. The following letters were exchanged between a mother and daughter over an incident at school:

My Dear Martha,
...you must kneel down and pray to God to keep you from sinning, and every night and morning you must do the same, for you will never be a good girl until He takes you into His keeping. It is because you have forgotten Him that you have been disobedient....

My Dearest Mother,
I have indeed been very wicked to distress you and my dear father as I have done....I have prayed to Christ to forgive me and love me once more, and I feel comforted now.

True to the times in which she lived, Charlotte's life was one of restraint, piety, and Christian virtue. The Brontë family was dedicated to these images. Maria Branwell Brontë was an extremely pious woman, and marrying the Reverend only magnified the religious issue. Charlotte was raised in this constraining atmosphere, yet her passionate nature and literary gifts enabled her to write an accurate tale of her times.

Jane Eyre was critically acclaimed in 1847 as "decidedly the best novel of the season," by G. H. Lewes in *The Westminster Review*. The Victorians respected the reality of the story, however, some critics thought it to be anti-Christian, and vulgar. Today, *Jane Eyre* endures as one of the most popular English novels, and is considered by some scholars to be the prototype of the feminist novel.

Master List Of Characters

Jane Eyre—*Protagonist and narrator of the story, orphaned, living with the Reed family when the story begins.*

Mrs. Sarah Reed—*Widow of Jane Eyre's uncle, mistress at Gateshead Hall.*

Eliza Reed—*Oldest daughter in the Reed family, cousin to Jane Eyre.*

John Reed—*Only son in the Reed family, a bully, cousin to Jane Eyre.*

Georgiana Reed—*Youngest daughter (the beauty) in the Reed family, cousin to Jane Eyre.*

Bessie Lee—*Servant at Gateshead Hall.*

Miss Abbot—*Servant at Gateshead Hall.*

Mr. Lloyd—*Apothecary who treats Jane at Gateshead Hall.*

Mr. Brocklehurst—*Minister of Brocklebridge Church, headmaster at Lowood School.*

Mr. Bates—*Doctor who treats Jane at Lowood School.*

Helen Burns—*Student at Lowood school who befriends Jane, and then dies of tuberculosis.*

Miss Miller—*An under-teacher at Lowood. She is in charge of Jane when Jane first arrives at Lowood School.*

Maria Temple—*Teacher at Lowood School.*

Miss Scatcherd—*Teacher at Lowood School.*

Mary Ann Wilson—*Jane's friend at Lowood School.*

John Eyre—*Jane's uncle, her father's brother.*

Edward Fairfax Rochester—*Master of Thornfield Hall; demanding, impatient, and passionate.*

Mrs. Alice Fairfax—*Housekeeper at Thornfield Hall, distant relative of Rochester by marriage.*

Celine Varens—*Former mistress of Mr. Rochester.*

Adele Varens—*Daughter of Celine, ward of Mr. Rochester, Jane's pupil.*

Leah—*Kitchen maid at Thornfield.*

John and Mary—*Servants at Thornfield.*

Grace Poole—*Caretaker of Bertha Rochester at Thornfield.*

Blanche Ingram—*The beautiful lady friend of Mr. Rochester.*

Richard (Dick) Mason—*Bertha Rochester's brother.*

Robert Leaven—*Bessie's husband.*

Mr. Briggs—*Solicitor who stops Jane's marriage to Mr. Rochester.*

Bertha Rochester—*Mad wife of Edward Rochester.*

Hannah—*Servant at Moor House.*

Diana and Mary Rivers—*Sisters of St. John Rivers.*

St. John Rivers—*Minister of the parish at Morton, master of Moor House; cold, strict, principled, and reserved.*

Rosamond Oliver—*Admires Mr. St. John Rivers, daughter of Mr. Oliver.*

Mr. Oliver—*Father of Rosamond.*

The Host—*Former butler of Edward Rochester's father, and the innkeeper of The Rochester Arms.*

Summary of the Novel

Jane Eyre, an orphan, lives with her abusive aunt, Sarah Reed, and her mean-spirited cousins, John, Eliza, and Georgiana, at Gateshead Hall.

She is sent away to the Lowood School where the conditions are very harsh. Jane befriends a fellow student, Helen Burns, and Miss Temple, a teacher. When Helen Burns dies, and Miss Temple marries, Jane decides to leave Lowood, and secures a job as a governess at Thornfield.

At Thornfield, Jane's duties are to teach the master's foster child Adele Varens. Although he has a brusque manner, Jane finds the master, Edward Fairfax Rochester, attractive and fascinating.

One night Jane is awakened by strange noises. Seeing smoke coming from Mr. Rochester's room, she runs in and throws water on the fire, awakening him. He leads Jane to believe that it is Grace Poole, a servant, who caused the damage.

Meanwhile, Mr. Rochester apparently pursues Blanche Ingram, a local beauty, while Jane's love for him continues to grow.

Jane leaves Thornfield to visit the dying Mrs. Reed, who tells her that John Eyre, her father's brother, is trying to contact her.

When Jane returns to Thornfield, Mr. Rochester switches his affections from Blanche to Jane, and proposes marriage. The wedding ceremony is interrupted by Mr. Briggs, who claims that Mr. Rochester is already married. The mad Bertha Rochester, who is locked away on the third floor of Thornfield, is exposed to Jane. Jane flees, and arrives at Moor House where she is taken in by St. John Rivers, a minister. Jane receives an inheritance from her uncle, John Eyre. St. John Rivers proposes marriage to Jane, but she declines since she still has Mr. Rochester on her mind.

Jane returns to Thornfield and discovers it has burned to the ground. It seems that Bertha Rochester set the fire and died in it, while Mr. Rochester suffered a mangled hand that had to be amputated and has been left blind. Jane reunites with Mr. Rochester at Ferndean, his current home, and they marry. Ten years pass, and Jane tells us how contented she is with married life, Mr. Rochester has regained partial vision in one eye, and they have a newborn son.

As an orphan, Jane's status is the lowest in the social class system. Because of her status (of which she is constantly reminded as a child) she strives to better herself through education and employment. During her struggles, Jane observes the other classes, including the religious zealots, with great insight and comes to recognize the many hypocrisies of the characters.

Emotionally, Jane is a lonely and ostracized child who recognizes her need for love and actively searches for it throughout her life, eventually finding her home with Mr. Rochester. Her search not only teaches her the true essence of love, but also enables her to raise her social position through hard work and the financial inheritance she receives.

Estimated Reading Time

Jane Eyre is divided into 38 chapters of varying length. It should take approximately 15 hours to read *Jane Eyre*.

SECTION TWO

Jane Eyre

Chapters I – III

New Characters:

Jane Eyre: *protagonist and narrator of the story, orphaned, living with the Reed family when the story begins*

Mrs. Sarah Reed: *widow of Jane Eyre's uncle, mistress at Gateshead Hall*

Eliza Reed: *oldest daughter in the Reed family, cousin to Jane Eyre*

John Reed: *only son in the Reed family, a bully, cousin to Jane Eyre*

Georgiana Reed: *youngest daughter (the beauty) in the Reed family, cousin to Jane Eyre*

Bessie: *servant at Gateshead Hall*

Miss Abbot: *servant at Gateshead Hall*

Mr. Lloyd: *apothecary who treats Jane at Gateshead Hall*

Summary

While Mrs. Reed and her children sit cozily by the fire, Jane is kept apart from the group and seeks refuge by reading a book in the window-seat of the breakfast room.

Fourteen-year-old John comes in and taunts Jane, scolds her for taking a book, and then throws it at her. Jane falls against a door and cuts her head, causing her to scream out at John that he

is a "wicked and cruel boy." John grabs her by the hair, and Jane swings at him, at which point the family enters and blames Jane for the incident. She is sent to the "Red Room."

Bessie and Miss Abbot try to calm Jane down, reminding her that if it weren't for Mrs. Reed, "you would have to go to the poor-house."

The Red Room is the room where Jane's uncle, Mr. Reed, died. Jane recollects her kind uncle and becomes very upset remembering the injustices thrust upon her. Suddenly, Jane sees a strange light, and imagines a ghost is in the room. She screams and sobs to be let out of the room, but Mrs. Reed keeps her locked in the Red Room. Jane falls to the floor, unconscious.

The next day Mr. Lloyd comes to examine her and suggests that Jane might be better off going away to school, and Mrs. Reed agrees. Overhearing a conversation between Miss Abbot and Bessie, Jane learns that her mother was disinherited for marrying a poor clergyman, and that both of her parents died of typhus when she was an infant.

Analysis

Several major themes of the novel are presented immediately: Jane Eyre's isolation; her struggle for her own survival under adverse conditions; her quest for and recognition of true Christian love; and the linking of a plain physical appearance with a favorable inner character, and a beautiful exterior with a defective character.

Brontë cleverly echoes Jane's feelings of isolation in the story Jane is reading, *History Of British Birds*. Physically separated from the family, Jane reads in her book, "the rock standing up alone in a sea of billow and spray; to the broken boat stranded on a desolate coast." The rock symbolizes Jane's own strength and endurance, the "desolate coast" symbolizes her bleak surroundings. Jane's experience is again echoed in the song Bessie sings to Jane— each verse ends in the line "poor orphan child."

Brontë introduces a writing device called the "pathetic fallacy," which she will use throughout the novel. Pathetic fallacy suggests parallel moods in nature to reflect the emotions of the characters. An example in these chapters is the weather described by Jane in the opening paragraph, "the cold winter wind had brought with it clouds so somber, and a rain so penetrating." Jane then sits in the window seat and tells the reader, "to the left were the clear panes of glass, protecting but not separating me from the drear November day....I studied the aspect of that winter afternoon. Afar, it offered a pale blank of mist and cloud; near, a scene of wet lawn and storm-beat shrub, with ceaseless rain sweeping away wildly before a long and lamentable blast." Nature is reflecting Jane's feelings, and also foreshadows the upcoming scene.

From the very beginning of the story, Jane calls on her inner strength to overcome adversity. She is constantly reminded of her orphan status—even the servants don't let her forget, "And you ought not to think yourself on equality with the Misses Reed and Master Reed," Miss Abbot informs her, going on to say, "God will punish her."

Rather than be beaten down by her struggle, Jane fights back, establishing her passionate nature. After her physical fight with John, Bessie exclaims, "Did ever anybody see such a picture of passion." Examples of her spunk are presented when she fights back after being hit by John, yells to be let out of the Red Room (red symbolizing passion), and tells Mr. Lloyd about her unhappiness.

The theme of Jane looking for a family and love is established when Jane muses, "I was in discord in Gatehead Hall; I was like nobody there; I had nothing in harmony with Mrs. Reed or her children, or her chosen vassalage. If they did not love me, in fact, as little did I love them."

It is in this hostile environment at Gateshead that Jane's quest for love begins. Mrs. Reed and the Reed children represent Christians who claim to be kind and loving yet exhibit cruel, hateful behavior.

Jane is extremely conscious of her physical appearance, expressing in the very first paragraph her "physical inferiority to her cousins." She describes her cousin Georgiana as being indulged and loved because of "her beauty, her pink cheeks, and golden curls." Bessie and Miss Abbot also concur that Jane would be better off if she were more attractive, physically. We later see that Jane has inner beauty, while the characters who are beautiful on the outside possess a flawed personality.

The story is told from the first-person point of view, beginning when Jane is a child of ten, and ending after she has been married for ten years. This device creates an intimacy between the reader and Jane.

Study Questions

1. Where does Jane live, and with whom?
2. What is her status, and how is she treated?
3. Why is Jane off reading alone?
4. Where is she sitting?
5. What happens between Jane and John?
6. What is Jane's reaction to being hit with the book?
7. How do we know that Mrs. Reed is an unkind woman?
8. How does Jane behave in the Red Room?
9. Why does Jane imagine a ghost or spirit?
10. How do we learn about Jane's appearance?

Answers

1. Jane lives at Gateshead hall with her aunt through marriage, Mrs. Reed, and her three cousins, John, Eliza, and Georgiana.
2. Jane is an orphan. She is treated very cruelly by Mrs. Reed and her children.
3. Mrs. Reed will not let Jane sit with the family.
4. Jane is sitting on a window seat in the breakfast room.
5. John throws a book at Jane, causing her head to bleed.
6. Jane hits John back and screams that he is "a wicked and cruel boy."
7. Mrs. Reed ejects Jane from the family circle, banishes her to the Red Room, and refuses to let her out when she sobs.
8. Jane reacts by working herself into a fit.
9. The Red Room is the room where Jane's uncle, Mr. Reed, has died. Jane also sees a light on the ceiling.

10. Both Bessie and Miss Abbot discuss Jane's plainness, and Jane compares herself unfavorably to her beautiful cousin Georgiana.

Suggested Essay Topics

1. Discuss how Jane's passionate nature is established.

2. Characterize Mrs. Reed, John Reed, Eliza, and Georgiana.

3. Explain first-person narrative, and why it might be beneficial to the story.

4. Discuss one, or more, of the themes that Brontë has established so far.

5. Explore the symbols that Brontë uses to enhance the story.

Chapters IV – VI

New Characters:

Mr. Brocklehurst: *minister of Brocklebridge Church, headmaster at Lowood School*

Miss Miller: *an under-teacher at Lowood School. She is in charge of Jane when Jane first arrives at Lowood*

Maria Temple: *teacher at Lowood School*

Helen Burns: *student at Lowood School who befriends Jane, and then dies of tuberculosis*

Miss Scatcherd: *teacher at Lowood School*

Summary

Jane endures a few more months at Gateshead Hall. Since her outburst, she is treated with more dislike from Mrs. Reed and is required to sleep in a small closet and take her meals alone. While the other children play, Jane is kept separate, and is hardly spoken to.

Excluded from all Christmas festivities, Jane finds solace alone with her doll; "To this crib I always took my doll; human beings must love something, and, in the dearth of worthier objects of affection, I contrived to find a pleasure in loving and cherishing a faded graven image, shabby as a miniature scarecrow. It puzzles me now to remember with what absurd sincerity I doted on this little toy, half fancying it alive and capable of sensation. I could not sleep unless it was folded in my night–gown; and when it lay there safe and warm, I was comparatively happy, believing it to be happy likewise."

An occasional kind word, and a gentle goodnight kiss from Bessie, are her only other comforts in this hostile environment.

Mr. Brocklehurst, the headmaster of Lowood School, comes to Gateshead Hall to meet with Jane. He interrogates Jane harshly, asking, "No sight so sad as that of a naughty child, especially a naughty little girl. Do you know where the wicked go after death?" When he asks Jane if she likes the Psalms, Jane, honest as always, replies, "No sir."

Mrs. Reed and Mr. Brocklehurst arrange for Jane to be sent to Lowood School. Mrs. Reed requests that Jane remain at Lowood even during vacations.

During her conversation with Mr. Brocklehurst, Mrs. Reed called Jane a liar, and Jane is very hurt by the remark. After Mr. Brocklehurst leaves, Jane and Mrs. Reed have a confrontation and Jane expresses her true feelings to her; "and if anyone asks me how I liked you, and how you treated me, I will say the very thought of you makes me sick, and that you treated me with miserable cruelty."

When Mrs. Reed defends herself, calls Jane a dear and tells her to lie down, Jane replies; "I am not your dear; I cannot lie down: send me to school soon, Mrs. Reed, for I hate to live here."

Jane is awakened at five o'clock on the morning of January 19 to travel the fifty miles to Lowood. She is greeted at Lowood by Miss Miller and Miss Temple.

At Lowood, Jane realizes quickly that this is a school for orphans, and the conditions are very harsh. Dinners of unappetizing stew, and snacks of thin cake or bread and water are shared amongst the eighty girls, and they all drink from a common mug. Breakfast is not much better, consisting of burnt porridge. The rooms are cold and dark, and the schedule is very regimented. The students' only enjoyment is a brief trip to the garden.

Jane sees Helen Burns sitting alone reading a book, and starts up a conversation. Helen tells Jane all that she knows about Lowood. The next day, Jane sees Helen beaten by Miss Scatcherd, and afterward, she engages Helen in conversation again. Helen's attitude surprises Jane. Rather than be bitter about the way she is treated, Helen expresses no resentment; instead she advocates Christ's teachings, "Love your enemies; bless them that curse you; do good to them that hate you and despitefully use you."

Jane replies, "Then I should love Mrs. Reed, which I cannot do; I should bless her son John, which is impossible."

Analysis

Jane's passionate nature is again expressed through her confrontation with Mrs. Reed. She is totally offended by being called a liar, when she knows she is not. When Jane cries out, "deceit is not my fault," Mrs. Reed exclaims, "but you are passionate, Jane." Rather than feel guilty for what she has said, Jane feels happy and liberated at first, then frightened. Later she shares her tea with Bessie, and is comforted by Bessie's songs. Bessie's attention is the only kindness Jane can count on.

At Lowood, Jane does not know what to expect. She is a keen observer of everything around her, but is too tired from her journey to worry much. Her status as an orphan is again emphasized when she discovers the sign calling Lowood an institution. She soon discovers that the abuse she has experienced is not going to end at Lowood.

Lowood is based on Brontë's experience at Cowan Bridge, the school where a typhus epidemic led to the death of her sisters. Jane describes in detail the morning meal, "I devoured a spoonful or two of my portion without thinking of its taste; but the first edge of hunger blunted, I perceived I had got in hand a nauseous mess: burnt porridge is almost as bad as rotten potatoes; famine itself soon sickens over it. The spoons were moved slowly: I saw each girl taste her food and try to swallow it; but in most cases the effort was soon relinquished. Breakfast was over, and none had breakfasted."

Besides not eating well, the girls were expected to go outside without warm clothing, "The stronger among the girls ran about and engaged in active games, but sundry pale and thin ones herded together for shelter and warmth in the veranda; and

amongst these, as the dense mist penetrated to their shivering frames, I heard frequently the sound of a hollow cough."

Jane sees a kindred spirit in Helen Burns because she notices her reading a book. Helen Burns is the symbol for true Christian love, even to the point of forgiving the people who abuse her. She not only believes in Christ's words but lives by them. Jane, on the other hand, cannot behave in a passive fashion because of her fiery nature.

Mr. Brocklehurst represents a hypocritical Christian. Although he quotes from the Bible, his actions are characteristically un-Christian. While professing love, he behaves cruelly.

For example, he explains to Mrs. Reed that "Humility is a Christian grace, and one peculiarly appropriate to the pupils of Lowood; I, therefore, direct that especial care shall be bestowed on its cultivation amongst them. I have studied how best to mortify in them the worldly sentiment of pride." However, his daughter's statements expose his hypocritical nature. She describes Lowood students. "They are almost like poor people's children! And, they looked at my dress and mamma's as if they had never seen a silk gown before." Obviously, Mr. Brocklehurst does not practice what he preaches for his own family.

Study Questions

1. How does Jane spend her last few months at Gateshead Hall?

2. What is Mr. Brocklehurst's attitude toward Jane?

3. What does Mrs. Reed tell Mr. Brocklehurst about Jane?

4. Why does Jane become upset at Mrs. Reed's statement?

5. What are the conditions at the Lowood School?

6. How would you characterize Miss Scatcherd?

7. Why does Jane think Helen Burns is approachable?

8. What shocks Jane about Helen?

9. How does Brontë use Helen as a symbol of Christian love?

10. How does Jane react to Helen's pious beliefs?

Answers

1. Jane continues to be excluded from the family's activities even during the Christmas holiday season.

2. Mr. Brocklehurst admonishes Jane for being naughty and reminds her that the wicked go to hell.

3. Mrs. Reed tells Mr. Brocklehurst that Jane has a tendency to deceit.

4. Jane becomes very upset because she knows herself to be an utterly truthful person.

5. At Lowood, the rooms were dark and cold, the meals were not nutritious, and basically inedible, and the treatment by most of the teachers was cruel.

6. Miss Scatcherd is a mean woman who consistently picks on Helen Burns and then beats her.

7. Jane realizes that she and Helen have a love of reading in common.

8. Jane is shocked that Helen is not resentful toward the people who are mean to her.

9. Helen recites Christ's teachings and honestly lives by his words.

10. Jane says it would be impossible for her to love Mrs. Reed or John Reed.

Suggested Essay Topics

1. Contrast the attitudes and behavior of Miss Temple and Miss Scatcherd.

2. Compare Jane's treatment at Gateshead Hall and at the Lowood School.

3. Discuss examples of Jane's passionate nature.

4. Explain how Brontë uses Helen Burns as a symbol of Christian goodness.

5. Describe a typical day at Lowood School.

Chapters VII – X

New Characters:

Mary Ann Wilson: *Jane's friend at Lowood School*

John Eyre: *Jane's uncle, her father's brother*

Summary

Jane's difficult existence at the Lowood School continues. She describes the insufficient meals, and how the poor clothing contributes to her sore feet at night after having to spend an hour outdoors in the cold without boots. On Sundays, they have to walk two miles in the cold to Brocklebridge Church, where cold meat and bread are served for dinner, before they have to walk the two miles back to school.

Mr. Brocklehurst comes to Lowood one day, demanding that the girls' hair be cut off and that they should not be offered cheese as snacks. He tells Miss Temple, "You are aware that my plan in bringing up these girls is not to accustom them to habits of luxury and indulgence, but to render them hardy, patient, self-denying." When his wife and daughter appear briefly, they are dressed and coifed elaborately and elegantly.

He then goes on to embarrass Jane in front of the whole school by telling them that she is a liar and they should not associate with her.

Jane's embarrassment over being called a liar in front of the whole school is soothed somewhat by a smile from Helen Burns. Although she weeps from this assault on her, Jane continues to work hard in her studies, and finds comfort from Helen, who tells her she "thinks too much of the love of human beings."

Miss Temple comes to her rescue by telling her she will write to Mr. Lloyd to confirm Jane's version of the story, and will announce to the class the truth. When the truth is told to the class, Jane is so relieved that she works extra hard on her studies.

She excels at her schoolwork and is promoted, which enables her to start classes in French, with the help of Madame Pierrot, and drawing. She sustains herself with the growing love she feels from Helen and Miss Temple.

The conditions at Lowood eventually lead to infections and illness for most of the girls, which alleviates the strict regime for a while. During this time Jane relies on a new friend, Mary Ann Wilson, for comfort since Helen Burns is also ill. Not really believing that Helen is near death, she sneaks into her room one night to visit with her. They hug and kiss and Jane falls asleep nestled in bed with Helen. Later on she is carried back to her room after being discovered by Miss Temple, and learns that Helen had died during the night.

Jane summarizes her last eight years at Lowood. After the typhoid epidemic, the conditions of the school were exposed and Mr. Brocklehurst was dismissed. In this new atmosphere, with Miss Temple as her companion and mentor, Jane thrives and eventually becomes a teacher. When Miss Temple decides to marry and leave Lowood, Jane realizes it is time for her to move on, and she places an advertisement in the newspaper.

Before she leaves, Bessie comes to visit her and brings her up-to-date on what's happening with the Reed family. She discloses to Jane that her father's brother, John Eyre, was looking for her several years ago. Jane accepts the job as governess and plans to move to Thornfield, in the town of Millcote. She is eighteen years old.

Analysis

Mr. Brocklehurst is explicitly shown to be a hypocrite. While his own family is dressed handsomely, he instructs the girls to have their hair cut off; "My mission is to mortify in these girls the lusts of the flesh; to teach them to clothe themselves with shamefacedness and sobriety, not with braided hair and costly apparel."

He scolds Miss Temple for giving them bread and cheese. "Oh Madam, when you put bread and cheese, instead of burnt porridge, into these children's mouths, you may indeed feed their vile bodies, but you little think how you starve their immortal souls!" His declarations of scripture heighten his hypocrisy, claiming he is doing this for the good of their souls, yet he is treating them with extreme cruelty.

Miss Temple represents goodness and fairness; caring for Jane and Helen with love under the dire circumstances. She invites

them to her room and gives them tea and seed cake. She believes Jane's version of her life at Gateshead, eventually clearing her reputation publicly.

Helen Burns is a good Christian whose death is poignantly described. Jane expresses her love and need for Helen, while Helen expresses her lack of fear over death, and proclaims her belief in God and the hereafter. "I am sure there is a future state; I believe God is good; I can resign my immortal part to Him without any misgiving. God is my father; God is my friend: I love Him; I believe He loves me."

After Mr. Brocklehurst is discharged from Lowood, Jane's life improves. She works hard at learning, and gains respect for her accomplishments. Through her education and artistic talent she is able to grow up to be self-assured and confident.

When Miss Temple leaves to marry, Jane knows she must also move on. Her desire for independence and strength of character is revealed again as she secretly pursues a job by placing an advertisement in the newspaper. Jane explains, "I desired liberty; for liberty I gasped; for liberty I uttered a prayer."

Bessie's visit before Jane leaves Lowood serves two purposes: Bessie admits to Jane that although the Reed girls are beautiful, they do not have her intelligence, and she calls John Reed "a dissipated young man," thus giving Jane some satisfaction. She also tells Jane that her father's brother, John Eyre, was looking for her several years ago, which hints to the reader and Jane that he may appear again.

Study Questions

1. What are the conditions at Lowood during the winter months?

2. How does Mr. Brocklehurst humiliate Jane?

3. Upon whom does Jane rely on for love and affection?

4. What happens at Lowood that changes the whole atmosphere?

5. How does Jane react after Miss Temple proves she is not a liar?

6. How does Helen view her impending death?

7. What happens to Jane during her last eight years at Lowood?

8. Why does Jane decide to leave Lowood?

9. How does she find other employment?

10. What news does Bessie bring her?

Answers

1. The children are half starved and sent out in the cold without warm clothing, and they must walk two miles to and from church on Sundays.

2. Mr. Brocklehurst tells the whole school that Jane is a liar, and instructs the students to shun her.

3. Helen Burns and Miss Temple give Jane some of the love she needs.

4. Most of the girls become sick with typhus, and Mr. Brocklehurst is dismissed.

5. Jane excels at her studies, and takes up French and drawing.

6. Helen accepts her death and looks forward to being in God's care.

7. Jane settles into the routine and eventually becomes a teacher.

8. After Miss Temple marries, Jane realizes she is ready for a change.

9. Jane puts an advertisement in the newspaper requesting a position as a teacher.

10. Bessie tells Jane that the Reed girls are not as intelligent as she, and that John is a disappointment to his mother. She also tells Jane that her uncle, John Eyre, had been looking for her several years earlier.

Suggested Essay Topics

1. Characterize Mr. Brocklehurst; include a physical description.

2. Describe the deathbed scene between Helen Burns and Jane. Explain Helen's philosophy.

3. Discuss Jane's behavior after Miss Temple reveals that she is not a liar.

4. Discuss Jane's need for a change after spending eight years at Lowood.

Chapters XI – XV

New Characters:

Edward Fairfax Rochester: *master of Thornfield Hall; demanding, impatient, and passionate*

Mrs. Alice Fairfax: *housekeeper at Thornfield Hall, distant relative of Rochester by marriage*

Celine Varens: *former mistress of Mr. Rochester*

Adele Varens: *daughter of Celine, ward of Mr. Rochester, Jane's pupil*

Leah: *kitchen maid at Thornfield Hall*

John and Mary: *servants at Thornfield Hall*

Grace Poole: *caretaker of Bertha Rochester at Thornfield*

Summary

Jane arrives at Thornfield Hall hoping that Mrs. Fairfax will not turn out to be like Mrs. Reed. She is pleasantly surprised to find her to be a warm and friendly person. In contrast to Lowood School, Thornfield Hall is a grand, yet comfortable house, where Jane has her own room. Mrs. Fairfax informs Jane that the master of house, Mr. Rochester, is often away, and explains to her that Adele, her pupil, is his ward and she is just the housekeeper.

Although she appreciates her new surroundings, and is genuinely fond of Adele, Jane is a little bored with her routine. "It is in vain to say human beings ought to be satisfied with tranquillity: they must have action; and they will make it if they cannot find it."

A strange, mysterious laugh is often heard throughout the house, and Jane is told by Mrs. Fairfax that it is "perhaps Grace Poole," a servant who sews and assists Leah with the housework.

One day while Jane is taking a two mile walk to the post office, she encounters a man whose horse has slipped on the ice. Jane describes her first reaction to Mr. Rochester. "He was past youth, but had not yet reached middle age; perhaps he might be thirty-five. I felt no fear of him, and but little shyness. Had he been a handsome, heroic-looking young gentleman, I should not have dared to stand thus questioning him against his will, and offering my services unasked." Jane goes on to explain his demeanor. "If even this stranger had smiled and been good-humored to me when I addressed him–if he had put off my offer of assistance gaily and with thanks, I should have gone on my way and not felt any vocation to renew inquiries; but the frown, the roughness of the traveler, set me at my ease."

Rochester questions Jane, and she reveals that she is the governess at Thornfield Hall, but he does not say who he is. Jane helps him to mount his horse, and continues on her way, not expecting to see this man again, but thinking about the new person she has just met.

When Jane returns to Thornfield she discovers that the man who fell on the ice was her new master, Mr. Rochester. The next night she is asked to dress for dinner and join Mrs. Fairfax, Adele, and Mr. Rochester. Mr. Rochester engages Jane in conversation and asks to see her paintings. At bedtime Jane questions Mrs. Fairfax about Mr. Rochester, and is told his strange nature is partly due to "family troubles, for one thing."

Jane busies herself tutoring Adele, but Mr. Rochester's presence is strongly felt. Several evenings later, he seeks Jane out again for conversation, and is a little surprised by Jane's candor. After noticing Jane looking at him, he asks if she thinks him handsome, and she answers, "No, sir."

Nevertheless he trusts Jane, and one afternoon while walking in the garden, he explains to her that Adele is the child of his "grande passion" Celine Varens, but that the child is not his. When Adele was abandoned by Celine, Mr. Rochester took her in as his ward.

One evening when everyone is sleeping Jane sees smoke coming from Mr. Rochester's room and runs in to awaken him. She finally throws water on him, and while he is shocked to see her there, he is thankful that she saved his life. He then leaves Jane waiting in the hall while he checks in the attic to see how the fire started.

It takes a while for him to come back, but when he does he asks Jane what she had seen. When he is assured that she has not seen anything, only heard that strange laugh of Grace Poole's, he dismisses the incident as Grace Poole's doing, and asks her not to mention it to anyone. Before going back to bed, he takes her hand and thanks her for saving his life.

Analysis

Jane begins a new phase of her life with her move to Thornfield Hall. Although her status has improved, her adventurous spirit longs for variety and stimulation in her daily life, and Mr. Rochester's appearance fulfills this need.

It is apparent from the onset that Jane and Mr. Rochester are kindred spirits. Both of them seem to have lived through tough times, yet they still manage to carry on with dignity and compassion for others.

Jane questions Mrs. Fairfax about Mr. Rochester and is told, "His character is unimpeachable, I suppose. He is rather peculiar." "In what way is he peculiar?" Jane asks. "I don't know—it is not easy to describe—nothing striking, but you feel it when he speaks to you; you cannot always be sure whether he is in jest or earnest, whether he is pleased or contrary; you don't thoroughly understand him, in short—at least, I don't: but it is of no consequence, he is a very good master." The fact that Rochester has also taken in Adele as his ward establishes his goodness.

Mr. Rochester is fascinated by Jane's integrity and strength, amazed that she endured eight years at Lowood, and he tells Jane, "Eight years! You must be tenacious of life." Their attachment begins with the verbal repartee in which they engage. Although Mr. Rochester's manner is direct and brusque, Jane is not intimidated, and replies to his inquiries with intelligence and confidence.

They each find the other mentally stimulating, but not physically attractive by classical standards. They are candid and direct

with each other. After answering "No, sir," to Rochester's question, "Do you think me handsome", Rochester goes on to say, "...you are not pretty any more than I am handsome, yet a puzzled look becomes you...."

This verbal banter is what excites each of them, filling the boredom they would otherwise experience. Rochester explains that he cannot talk to only children and servants. He is energized by Jane's verbal spunk. "I mentally shake hands with you for your answer....Not three in three thousand raw school-girl governesses would have answered me as you have done."

Unlike the behavior of a typical Victorian woman, Jane's conversation is brutally honest, and Rochester appreciates this trait in her most of all. He compares her to his unfaithful mistress Celine; after telling Jane about discovering Celine with another man, he says, "Wherein she differed diametrically from you, who told me point-blank that you did not think me handsome. The contrast struck me at the time."

Rather than be shocked by Rochester's story, Jane continues to be fascinated by him, and embraces Adele more so. Her compassion for the child deepens, she tells Rochester. "I have a regard for her, and now I know she is in a sense, parentless–forsaken by her mother and disowned by you, sir–I shall cling closer to her than before."

The mysterious laugh, and the fire, blamed on Grace Poole keeps Jane curious, and alerts the reader to recognize that all is not what it seems at Thornfield Hall.

Jane comes to Rochester's rescue twice in this section. First, she helps him back onto his horse not knowing who he is, and then she saves him from the fire in his bedroom. It is apparent to the reader, now, that Rochester is more than a little interested in Jane and that Jane is quickly falling in love with him. When he takes her hand after the fire incident, Jane spends the rest of the evening "too feverish to rest, I rose as soon as day dawned."

Study Questions

1. How did Jane first meet Mr. Rochester?

2. Describe Mrs. Fairfax's personality.

3. Explain Jane's identification with Adele.

4. What is Jane's mood when Mr. Rochester comes home?

5. What intrigues Mr. Rochester about Jane?

6. What do Jane and Mr. Rochester think about each other's appearance?

7. Why does Jane think Grace Poole odd?

8. Explain the circumstances that ended the relationship between Celine Varens and Mr. Rochester.

9. Why is Jane's knowledge of French important to her now?

10. How does Jane react to having her hand held by Mr. Rochester?

Answers

1. Jane meets Mr. Rochester on the road when his horse slips on the ice.

2. Mrs. Fairfax is a warm and friendly person. She is very happy to have Jane join the staff at Thornfield.

3. Jane likes Adele immediately, but cares even more for her when she finds out that she is an orphan like herself.

4. Jane is feeling rather bored and restless.

5. Mr. Rochester is fascinated by her strength and honesty.

6. Jane does not think Rochester handsome, and he thinks Jane to be plain.

7. She believes her to be the person with the strange laugh and the one who started the fire.

8. Celine brought another man to her bedroom, and Mr. Rochester overheard them discussing him in a negative way.

9. Adele speaks mostly French and very little English.

10. Jane cannot sleep for the rest of the night, and describes herself as feeling feverish.

Suggested Essay Topics

1. Compare the environment at Thornfield Hall to the Lowood School.

2. Examine how Jane has come to the rescue of Mr. Rochester.

3. Explain how the mysterious laugh leads Jane and the reader to know that all is not what it seems at Thornfield Hall.

4. Discuss Jane and Mr. Rochester's growing attraction.

5. Identify and discuss the symbols in Jane's artwork.

Chapters XVI – XIX

New Characters:

Blanche Ingram: *the beautiful lady friend of Mr. Rochester*

Richard (Dick) Mason: *Bertha Rochester's brother*

Summary

Mr. Rochester continues to occupy Jane's thoughts. She wakes up thinking, "I wanted to hear his voice again, yet I feared to meet his eye." When she encounters Grace Poole, she is completely puzzled by her, and cannot quite understand why she is not reprimanded for her behavior.

Jane looks forward to seeing Mr. Rochester again, but is told that he has gone away for awhile. During this time she hears a good deal of gossip about Blanche Ingram from Mrs. Fairfax. Afterwards, she admonishes herself for thinking that Mr. Rochester might care for her, knowing that she cannot compete with a lady as beautiful as Blanche. She draws portraits of her plain face and Blanche's beautiful one and vows to put Rochester from her thoughts. Mr. Rochester comes back from his trip early with a number of visitors, and plans evening entertainment.

Included with his visitors is Blanche Ingram. Jane takes a special interest in observing Blanche, knowing of Rochester's interest in her. "The noble bust, the sloping shoulders, the graceful neck, the dark eyes and black ringlets, were all there;–but her

face?...She laughed continually: her laugh was satirical, and so was the habitual expression of her arched and haughty lip."

Jane concludes from her observations, "Miss Ingram was a mark beneath jealousy: she was too inferior to excite the feeling. Pardon the seeming paradox: I mean what I say. She was very showy, but she was not genuine: she had a fine person, many brilliant attainments: but her mind was poor, her heart barren by nature; nothing bloomed spontaneously on that soil; no unforced natural fruit delighted by its freshness. She was not good; she was not original: she used to repeat sounding phrases from books; she never offered, nor had, an opinion of her own."

Jane is not jealous of Blanche, but angry, because she knows that Mr. Rochester does not truly love Blanche. However, she accepts that people like Mr. Rochester must marry for social reasons and to gain family connection.

Blanche's temperament is further exposed when she calls Adele a "tiresome monkey," because Adele had mistaken Richard Mason for Mr. Rochester.

Although Rochester's attention is on Blanche Ingram, he is aware of Jane's every move. When she tries to slip out of the parlor to go to bed, Rochester catches her and inquires why she looks so depressed. Jane denies that she is depressed. "I am tired, sir," she explains.

A few nights later, Rochester dresses up as a gypsy and gives fortune-telling sessions to his guests without revealing his identity. Blanche exits the room annoyed, and sits down with a book, but never reads it. "She never turned a page, and her face grew momently darker, more dissatisfied, and more sourly expressive of disappointment."

When it is Jane's turn, she reacts haughtingly to Rochester's questions. When he asks her, "I wonder with what feelings you came to me tonight....I wonder what thoughts are in your heart," Jane answers, "I feel tired often, sleepy sometimes, but seldom sad." He continues to probe, but Jane does not divulge any information. She had already admitted to herself that she loves Mr. Rochester, after watching his interactions with Blanche, but never lets on to the gypsy.

Jane then feels herself listening to the voice as if in a dream. "Where was I? Did I wake or sleep? Had I been dreaming? Did I dream still?" She then recognizes the voice as Rochester's and notices his ring.

When Rochester reveals his identity to Jane, he wants her to stay and talk to him about what is going on in the other room. She wants to leave, but before she goes, she tells him that a stranger, Mr. Mason, has arrived. At this news, Rochester gets very upset and asks to lean on Jane for support.

Analysis

The mystery of Grace Poole is explored through Jane's curiosity. The novel shows Jane's and Rochester's growing attraction to each other.

When Jane hears about Blanche Ingram, she feels herself to be physically and socially inferior to Blanche, and instructs herself to calm her feelings about Rochester. When she first observes the guests, Jane compares herself unfavorably to them also, dwelling on their height and elegance.

However, after observing Blanche, Jane finds her to be a phony and asserts that Rochester couldn't possibly love her. She feels he must be marrying her for political reasons.

While watching Blanche and Rochester interact, Jane has to admit, "I have told you reader, that I had learnt to love Mr. Rochester; I could not unlove him now."

Jane continues to fascinate Rochester, and there are many indications of his growing love for her. He seeks out her companionship even while entertaining house guests, and notices her feelings, commenting on her depression. He almost slips and uses endearing words, "Goodnight my ____," before biting his lip and going to bed.

When playing the gypsy, he tries to get her to reveal her feelings, and then describes her with acute insight, "...that brow professes to say, I can live alone, if self-respect and circumstances require me so to do. I need not sell my soul to buy bliss. I have an inward treasure born with me, which can keep me alive if all extraneous delights should be withheld, or offered only at a price I cannot afford to give."

We again see Rochester leaning on Jane, for physical support, after hearing Richard Mason's name. This physical gesture represents his growing emotional need for her. She's always there to rescue him, and he obviously has put his trust in her. He verbalizes his fantasies—"I wish I were in a quiet island with only you,"—a dramatically romantic admission.

Another mysterious character is presented; Richard Mason. Other than being described as a friend from the West Indies, it is not explained who he is, but Jane takes an immediate dislike to him. The chapter ends with Rochester almost keeling over when hearing his name. He tells Jane, "I've got a blow;–I've got a blow, Jane!" to which she replies, "Oh–lean on me, sir."

Study Questions

1. What effect has Mr. Rochester had on Jane?

2. Why does she want to suppress her feelings?

3. How does Jane react to Mr. Mason?

4. Why is she so curious about Grace Poole?

5. What does she observe about Blanche?

6. How does Rochester try to keep Jane involved in the festivities?

7. What does he observe about her feelings?

8. How do we know Jane is more clever than the other guests?

9. What reaction does Rochester have when he learns that Richard Mason has arrived?

10. What is the significance of Jane being able to physically support Rochester, again?

Answers

1. Jane admits to loving Rochester.

2. She believes she cannot compete with Blanche Ingram, who is described as being beautiful, and socially prominent.

3. Jane takes an immediate dislike to him.

4. Believing Grace to be the person who caused the fire, and who mysteriously laughs, Jane does not understand why Grace is allowed to get away with her behavior.

5. After observing Blanche interact with the other guests, Jane concludes that she is a phony, and that Mr. Rochester could not possibly love her. She assumes it is a political arrangement.

6. Rochester insists on her attendance at the events, and asks where she is going when she attempts to leave.

7. He tells her she looks depressed, though Jane denies it.

8. Jane recognizes Rochester under the gypsy costume, although he apparently fooled the rest of the guests.

9. He becomes very distressed and leans on Jane for support.

10. This gesture represents his growing emotional need for her, and Jane's constant presence as his helper.

Suggested Essay Topics

1. Discuss how the mystery of Grace Poole is perpetuated.

2. Brontë has Jane give detailed descriptions of the physical appearance of the characters; compare and contrast the physical appearance of Jane with Blanche Ingram.

3. Discuss evidence of Rochester's growing love for Jane.

4. Characterize Edward Rochester; include physical descriptions.

Chapters XX – XXII

New Character:

Robert Leaven: *Bessie's husband*

Summary

During the night, everyone awakens to a loud cry and a sharp sound. Rochester calms everyone down, but summons Jane to the attic to help him. There she discovers Richard Mason soaked in blood, apparently stabbed. Rochester instructs Jane to nurse him and stay with him for at least an hour or two, and demands that they not speak to each other. "Richard–it will be at the peril of your

life if you speak to her: open your lips–agitate yourself–and I'll not answer for the consequences." When leaving the room, Rochester says again, "Remember!–No conversation."

Jane is frightened of the person ranting in the next room, assuming it to be Grace Poole. Richard Mason describes his attacker as a raging animal; he says he was bit before he was stabbed. The mystery deepens; Jane cannot understand the relationship between Richard Mason and Rochester, she wonders why Mason was submissive to Rochester's demands, and why Rochester reacted so strongly when he heard of Richard's arrival. After Jane helps Rochester move Richard Mason to a waiting carriage, he invites her to the garden to chat, and they sit together on a bench.

He begins telling Jane a parable by asking her to imagine or "suppose", you were a " wild boy" in a "remote foreign land", who commits an "error, not a crime", and then travels the world seeking solace in "heartless, sensual pleasure", until he returns to his home and meets a " stranger much of the good and bright qualities which you have sought for twenty years." Would she be willing to "overleaping an obstacle of custom–a mere conventional impediment," in order to lead a life "worthy of immortal being"?

Jane is dumbfounded by the question, and speechless. Rochester phrases the question in another way and Jane answers, "A wanderer's repose or a sinner's reformation should never depend on a fellow creature. Men and women die; philosophers falter in wisdom, and Christians in goodness: if any one you know has suffered and erred, let him look higher than his equals for strength to amend and solace to heal."

Rochester ends their conversation by describing Blanche Ingram's assets, and urges Jane to sit up with him the night before his marriage. "Will you promise to sit up with me to bear me company? To you I can talk of my lovely one: for now you have seen her and know her." "Yes, sir," Jane answers. Rochester continues, "She's a rare one, is she not, Jane?" "Yes, sir," Jane replies.

Jane begins having dreams of an infant and remembers how Bessie used to say that dreaming of children was a sign of trouble. Soon after, Robert Leaven comes to Thornfield to summon Jane to visit the dying Mrs. Reed, who has asked to see her. He also tells Jane that John Reed is dead, the talk is he killed himself.

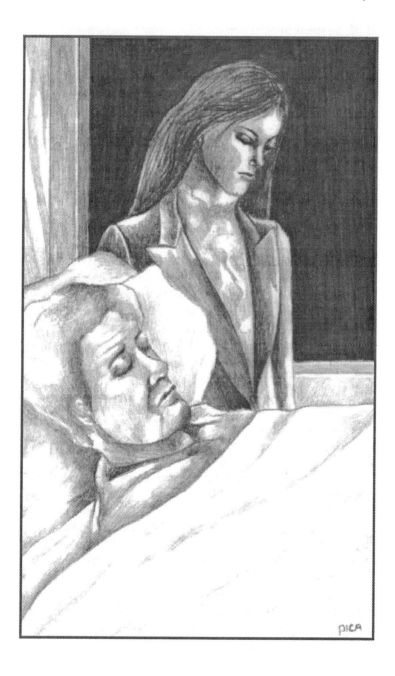

Jane agrees to travel the one hundred miles to Gateshead and asks Rochester for permission to leave. He is surprised that she has family; he thought her to be totally alone. Jane then requests that he find proper schooling for Adele, and she will have to find a new position in light of his upcoming marriage. He asks her to promise that she will not advertise for a new position, that he will take care of it.

Jane goes to Gateshead and finds the dying Mrs. Reed, unchanged after all these years. Jane, however, explains how she had left Gateshead with a "desperate and embittered heart," but she has returned, "quite healed, and the flame of resentment extinguished."

Mrs. Reed, in a delirious state, tells Jane that she has always hated her; she had hated Jane's mother and was jealous of the attention her husband, Mr. Reed, showed Jane as an infant. When the typhus epidemic broke out at Lowood, Mrs. Reed says, she wished Jane had died.

Ten days pass, and Jane spends time with Georgiana and Eliza. Eliza is a rigid church goer, and retreats from conversation. Georgiana is plump, lazy, talks about herself constantly and complains of being bored. The sisters bicker and Eliza tells Georgiana, "After my mother's death I wash my hands of you."

Jane goes to Mrs. Reed's room on a wet and windy afternoon, and it seems that Mrs. Reed wants to relieve her conscience. She admits to Jane that she has done her wrong two times: "One time was breaking the promise which I gave my husband to bring you up as my own child," she says, and then stops. She asks Jane to get a letter from her drawer and tells Jane to read it. The letter, dated three years ago, was from her uncle, John Eyre. The uncle was alone and had come into some money. He wished to adopt Jane, "during my life, and bequeath her at my death whatever I may have to leave." Keeping the letter secret was the second wrong.

Mrs. Reed explains that she never told Jane about the letter because she had always disliked her and couldn't forget Jane's rude conduct toward her. For revenge, she wrote to John Eyre and told him that Jane had died of typhus at the Lowood School. Mrs. Reed could not bear to see Jane fixed in a comfortable position. In spite of this admission, Jane responds, "You have my full and free for-giveness: ask now for God's, and be at peace."

Mrs. Reed dies alone, without her daughters at her side. Jane stays with Georgiana and Eliza a few weeks, to help them settle their belongings, and then goes back to Thornfield Hall. The cous-ins' histories are summarized and then projected into the future. Eliza becomes a nun, and Georgiana marries a worn-out, fash-ionable, wealthy man.

Jane anticipates her reunion with Rochester with great excite-ment, exclaiming how she had never felt this way about returning home before, although Thornfield is not really her home. She ad-mits it is Rochester she looks forward to seeing, in spite of the fact that he is not interested in her, "but you know very well you are thinking of another than they; and that he is not thinking of you."

When she does see Rochester again, she cannot control the impulse to admit to him, "I am strangely glad to get back again to you; and wherever you are is my home–my only home."

Jane finds herself grieving over the prospect of Rochester marrying Blanche Ingram, but she observes no preparations for the event, and begins to have hope that perhaps the engagement is off. Rochester, in turn, is behaving surprisingly "gay," as Jane describes, "Never had he called me more frequently to his pres-ence; never been kinder to me when there–and alas! never had I loved him so well."

Analysis

There is much information packed into these chapters, and much emotion. Jane's love for Rochester has reached a peak, while the mystery of Grace Poole continues. A new mystery is added: how does Richard Mason figure in this?

Rochester gives hints of his affection for Jane, but Jane can't be sure of his feelings because of his upcoming wedding to Blanche Ingram.

In addition, her childhood has come back to haunt her; she is called back to Gateshead Hall by Mrs. Reed on her deathbed. During this visit, she discovers that Georgiana is still vain and self-ish, Eliza is retreating, and Mrs. Reed is still an embittered per-son; she dies alone without any comfort or love.

All of the Reeds seem to get what they deserve; thus Brontë introduces the theme of retribution.

The crucial information presented here to Jane is that she indeed has an uncle who wanted to adopt her and was looking for her three years ago. Jane proves her Christian attitude by forgiving Mrs. Reed for all of her abuse, while Mrs. Reed, in contrast, remains mean, embittered, and unloved.

When Jane leaves Gateshead Hall, she knows she will never see Georgiana or Eliza Reed again and tells the reader their future whereabouts: Georgiana weds a wealthy man, and Eliza enters a convent.

As Jane is approaching Thornfield Hall, she is practically delirious with the excitement of seeing Rochester again. When she sees him she blurts out her emotions, and then walks quickly away. Afterwards Rochester seems happy, or "gay," as Jane describes him. No preparations are being made for the supposed wedding to Blanche.

Study Questions

1. What is the added mystery in this chapter?

2. How is Rochester's behavior contradictory?

3. What has happened to John Reed?

4. What important information does Mrs. Reed tell Jane?

5. Who is with Mrs. Reed when she dies?

6. How is the attacker described by Richard Mason?

7. What becomes of Georgiana and Eliza Reed?

8. How does Jane feel when she is approaching Thornfield Hall?

9. What does she blurt out to Rochester?

10. How does Jane describe him?

Answers

1. Richard Mason is attacked by someone in the attic.

2. Rochester intimates his love for Jane, but proceeds with his plans to marry Blanche.

3. John Reed apparently drank himself into debt, eventually using up his mother's money as well. The rumor is that he killed himself.

4. Mrs. Reed tells Jane of her uncle, John Eyre, who three years earlier sought to make Jane his heir. Mrs. Reed told him that Jane had died of typhus at Lowood.

5. Nobody is with Mrs. Reed, she dies alone.

6. Richard Mason describes his attacker as an animal who bit him and sucked his blood.

7. Georgiana goes on to make a prestigious match, and Eliza enters the convent.

8. She is extremely excited about seeing Rochester again; she talks about how she had never felt like this, as if she were coming home.

9. She tells Rochester that anywhere he is, is her home.

10. She describes him as being very happy.

Suggested Essay Topics

1. Discuss how the mystery becomes more intriguing.

2. Explain the element of foreshadowing in Jane's dream about the infant.

3. Analyze Rochester's contradictory behavior; why is Jane confused?

4. Discuss Jane's declaration of love for Rochester.

Chapters XXIII – XXV

Summary

Jane takes a walk in the garden on a mid-summer night, and the smell of Rochester's cigar lets Jane know that he is near. She tries to avoid him, but he summons her into the orchard where they begin discussing his upcoming wedding.

When he suggests that she might take a governess job in Ireland, Jane tells him, "It's a long way off, sir?" "From what, Jane," he asks, and she replies, "From, you, sir," and starts to cry.

Rochester admits, "I sometimes have a queer feeling with regard to you–especially when you are near me, as now: it is as if I had a string somewhere under my left ribs, tightly and inextricably knotted to a similar string situated in the corresponding quarter of your little frame."

When Jane responds by telling him, that in spite of her grief she must leave because of his bride, Rochester says, "I have no bride."

In an impassioned speech Jane then reveals, "Do you think I can stay to become nothing to you? Do you think I am an automaton?–a machine without feelings?...Do you think because I am poor, obscure, plain, and little, I am soulless and heartless? You think wrong!–I have as much soul as you. I am not talking to you now through the medium of custom, conventionalities, nor even of mortal flesh–it is my spirit that addresses your spirit; just as if both had passed through the grave, and we stood at God's feet, equal,–as we are!"

Rochester responds by repeating, "As we are!" and gathers her in his arms and kisses her. Jane tries to pull away, struggling, as Rochester says, "like a frantic wild bird." She pulls away responding, "I am no bird; and no net ensnares me."

Rochester makes his proposal. "I offer you my hand, my heart, and a share of all my possessions." Jane thinks he is merely making a joke. He tells Jane to listen to the nightingale, and she again breaks down and sobs. Rochester tries to soothe her, and tells her, "But, Jane, I summon you as my wife; it is you only I intend to marry."

She still thinks he is mocking her. "Your bride stands between us," Jane responds. Rochester says, "My bride is here, because my equal is here, and my likeness. Jane will you marry me?" Seeing that Jane still doubts him, Rochester explains, "What love have I for Miss Ingram? None–and that you know. What love has she for me? None–as I have taken to prove. I cause a rumor to reach her that my fortune was not a third of what was supposed; and after that I presented myself to see the result: it was coldness both from her and her mother."

His next passionate declaration nearly convinces Jane. "I would not–I could not marry Miss Ingram. You–you strange, you almost unearthly thing!–I love as my own flesh. You–poor and obscure, and small and plain as you are–I entreat to accept me as a husband."

Jane wants to see his expression in the moonlight. "Why?" Rochester asks. "Because I want to read your countenance," says Jane. He begs her to accept quickly, "for I suffer." She finally believes him, and accepts his proposal, calling him, "Dear Edward," before being pulled into his arms.

A storm is approaching and they both get soaked in the rain before hurrying into Thornfield. Inside, Rochester holds Jane in his arms and kisses her repeatedly, after shaking off her wet hair, and removing her wet shawl. Mrs. Fairfax unexpectedly comes out of her room and observes this display of affection.

Jane goes off to bed, and first thing in the morning she is told by Adele that the huge horse chestnut tree in the orchard has been split in half by lighting.

Jane is still a little dazzled in the morning, wondering if it might all have been a dream. When she observes herself in the mirror, she thinks she is not as plain, and has never looked so good because, "none had I ever worn in so blissful a mood. "

When she goes to breakfast, Mrs. Fairfax is a little cool toward her. Rochester beckons her and greets her with an embrace and a kiss, reassuring Jane that it is not a dream. When he explains how he will send for heirloom jewels for her to wear, she tells him that jewels would be unnatural for her. "I am your plain, Quakerish governess."

When Rochester goes on to protest that she is beautiful to him, he will attire her in satin and lace, and "I will cover the head I love best with a priceless veil," Jane responds by saying, "And then you won't know me, sir; and I shall not be your Jane Eyre any longer, but an ape in a harlequin's jacket–a jay in borrowed plumes."

Jane corners Rochester into responding to the one thing she wants to know; why did he pretend to want to marry Miss Ingram? Rochester tells Jane that it was to make her jealous, and to get her to love him as much as he loved her.

Jane also asks Rochester to explain to Mrs. Fairfax about their engagement before she sees her again. She does not want Mrs. Fairfax to misjudge her.

After being initially shocked by the engagement, saying to Jane, "Miss Eyre, I have surely not been dreaming, have I?" Mrs. Fairfax accepts the news, but advises Jane that "all is not gold that glitters."

Rochester takes Jane on a shopping spree, but she buys the plainer material for her dresses and is anxious to get him out of the shops. "The more he bought me, the more my cheek burned with a sense of annoyance and degradation," Jane says.

That evening he summons her to sit up with him, but she avoids intimacy by having him sing a song to her, and then saying a hasty goodnight. He calls her hard, and she admits that for all her firmness, "my task was not an easy one; often I would rather have pleased than teased him. My future husband was becoming to me my whole world; and more than the world: almost my hope of heaven."

A month passes and the wedding is set for the next day. Jane can't seem to control her nerves; Mr. Rochester had been away for the night, and anticipating his return she goes into the orchard and wanders around. She observes the horse chestnut tree. "It stood up, black and riven: the trunk, split down the center, gasped ghastly. The cloven halves were not broken from each other, for the firm base and strong roots kept them unsundered below; though community of vitality was destroyed– the sap could flow no more: their great boughs on each side were dead, and next winter's tempests would be sure to fell one or both to earth; as yet, however they might be said to form one tree–a ruin, but an entire ruin."

With the wind roaring, Jane walks down to the gate and meets Rochester returning home; he sweeps her up onto the horse.

That night Jane has a vivid dream that she is carrying a baby on the grounds of Thornfield Hall, but the mansion has been re-duced to ruins. She sees Rochester in the distance retreating on his horse. She awakens with a start and finds a dark-haired, red-eyed woman in her room trying on her wedding veil. She's not sure if it is real or part of the dream.

She describes her fearful dream to Rochester and he calms her by saying it was part dream, part reality. She asks him to explain the strange mystery of Mrs. Poole; he promises to tell her in a year's time. He tells her she should sleep with Adele that night in order to sleep serenely.

Jane retires unable to sleep, clutching Adele to her.

Analysis

The mystery and the love affair are brought to a climax in these chapters. Jane and Rochester both make passionate declarations of their love. Jane's initial statements of passion convince Rochester of her love, and when he finally lets down his guard, he explodes with his feelings. They refer to each other as "equals."

Although it would seem that all of Jane's troubles end with the marriage proposal, Jane can't seem to accept the idea without fear. She has another nightmare where she is holding a baby, and sees Thornfield Hall in ruins.

The dream is heightened when she awakens to see the mad-woman in her room. The fact that the mad-woman puts on the wedding veil indicates something unknown or frightening is connected to the wedding. Jane has trouble putting tags on her luggage with the name Mrs. Rochester. "I could not persuade myself to affix them, or to have them affixed. Mrs. Rochester! She did not exist."

Jane refers to the word, "dream," often throughout these passages. She is having trouble understanding the difference between her dreams and reality. Jane's dreams work as a foreshadowing of future events. We know that Jane's dreams are important; the last time she was summoned to Gateshead, by the dying Mrs. Reed.

The suspense and mystery build when the mad–woman enters Jane's room. We know that all of this anxiety must lead to a revelation of some sort, and it is connected somehow to the upcoming marriage.

The device of prophetic fallacy is vividly used in this section. Many symbols are evident: the walk in the orchard garden reflecting the beauty of Rochester and Jane's love; the violent thunderstorm reflecting their passionate natures, and that trouble lies ahead; and the horse–chestnut tree, symbolizing Rochester and Jane, united and strong, but eventually splitting in half, suggesting or foreshadowing a future catastrophe.

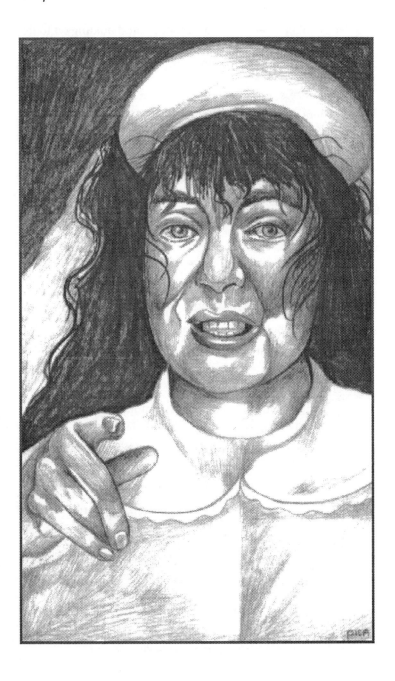

Jane explains her sleeping with Adele and holding on to her as "the emblem of my past life." The reader knows that Jane will now leave her childhood behind her.

Study Questions

1. Where and at what time of the year and day does Rochester's proposal take place?

2. What prompts him to propose?

3. How does Jane react at first?

4. Why are they forced to run into the house after the proposal?

5. How does Jane respond to Rochester's offer of jewels and fancy clothes?

6. What warning does Mrs. Fairfax give Jane?

7. How do Jane's fears show up in her dreams?

8. Who wakes Jane from her fitful sleep?

9. What happens to the chestnut tree?

10. Where does Jane sleep on the eve of her wedding?

Answers

1. It is mid-summer when Rochester proposes. They are in the orchard at night.

2. Jane passionately reveals her true feelings, calling them "equals."

3. Jane is shocked; she thinks he is just playing a joke on her.

4. A violent thunderstorm breaks out, so they run into the house.

5. She tells him it would not become her, she would not be "Jane Eyre."

6. Mrs. Fairfax warns Jane that "all is not gold that glitters."

7. She dreams once more of an infant and sees Thornfield Hall in ruins.

8. The mad, mystery woman enters Jane's room.

9. The tree is split in two by a lightning bolt.

10. Jane spends the night with Adele, and is unable to sleep.

Suggested Essay Topics

1. Discuss how suspense is built in these three chapters.

2. Explain why Jane does not want to be lavished with expensive gifts.

3. Point out examples of symbolism; how do they fit into the story?

Chapters XXVI – XXVII

New Characters:

Mr. Briggs: *a lawyer who stops Jane's marriage to Mr. Rochester*

Bertha Rochester: *mad wife of Edward Rochester*

Summary

On the morning of the wedding, Jane is taking her time dressing, while Rochester is impatiently waiting. He hurries her into the carriage and to the church. As they walk through the graveyards, Jane spots unfamiliar faces off in the distance.

Just when the priest is asking Rochester to repeat his wedding vow, a voice pops up saying there are "impediments" to the marriage. The ceremony is stopped and a lawyer steps forward to read a letter, stating that Mr. Rochester already has a wife; he had been married fifteen years ago. The letter is sighed by Richard Mason, and he subsequently presents himself.

Rochester defends himself, explaining that he was not really becoming a bigamist, and that Jane is innocent; she did not have any knowledge of his wife.

He leads the group back to Thornfield Hall and up to the attic into the chamber. There sits Grace Poole guarding her charge. The door is opened to reveal the mad-woman. "A fierce cry seemed to give the lie to her favorable report: the clothed hyena rose up, and stood tall on its hind feet....The maniac bellowed; she parted her

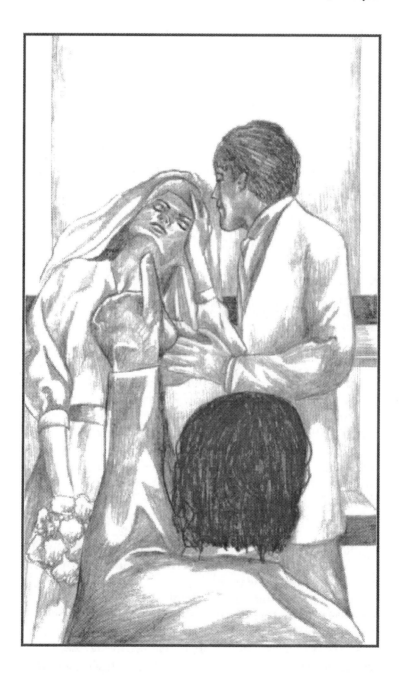

shaggy locks from her visage, and gazed wildly at her visitors. I recognized well that purple face, those bloated features." The madwoman turns out to be the first wife of Rochester, and the sister of Richard Mason.

Jane locks herself in her room. She doesn't cry, but mechanically takes off the wedding dress and after reviewing the circumstances presented, comes to the conclusion that she must leave Thornfield Hall.

Sometime in the afternoon, realizing she has not been summoned for hours, Jane comes out of her room feeling faint, and Rochester catches her fall. Rochester had been sitting in a chair outside her room. He apologizes profusely, and Jane forgives him, but stands firm in her decision to leave. Rochester says he'll send Adele to school and have his wife cared for, but he still cannot convince Jane to stay. He offers to take her as his wife and move to the South of France, but Jane refuses.

In trying to convince Jane to stay, Rochester explains the circumstances of his first marriage. It seems his father left all his property to Rochester's brother, but arranged a marriage for Rochester into a wealthy West Indian family. Everyone knew that there was insanity in the family, but no one ever told Rochester. Therefore, he felt swindled, and tried to deal as best he could with the situation.

After Rochester discovers Bertha's madness, he is at a point of suicide, until a "...true Wisdom consoled me in that hour, and showed me the right path to follow." He tells Jane that Europe was beckoning him, and how he had taken Bertha back to Thornfield, where he installed her in the third floor, and "whose secret inner chamber she has now for ten years made a wild beast's den–a goblin's cell."

He admits to setting Bertha up at Thornfield, and then going out to find himself a real wife. He openly discusses his mistresses with Jane, explaining how he gave them all up for his Jane. Jane is moved by his passion, but she does not give in.

When he sits down and cries, Jane runs to his side before rushing off to her room to rest. She's awakened by her mother's voice telling her, "My daughter, flee temptation." "Mother I will," Jane answers.

It is around midnight when Jane takes a small bag and tip-toes past Rochester's room. She can hear him pacing.

She slips out and travels in the opposite direction of Millcote. She thanks God for her strength, but is deeply grief-stricken and totally alone.

After spending two nights walking for miles and sleeping in damp fields, Jane arrives, delirious, on a road, and flags down a passing coach. She pays the driver to take her to the town where he is going, and rides alone to some unknown destiny. Her destitution is expressed in her final impassioned speech to the reader: "Gentle reader, may you never feel what I then felt! May your eyes never shed such stormy, scalding, heart-wrung tears as poured from mine."

Analysis

The mystery is exposed in this chapter and Jane is confronted with the information the reader has already guessed. Jane's anxieties and dreams have proven prophetic.

While Jane admits to still loving Rochester completely, her mind tells her that she must leave Thornfield Hall. When she sleeps, she dreams she is a child back at Gateshead. Her mother's voice wakes her, telling her to flee.

It takes all of Jane's strength to leave the only adult love she's ever known, but she cannot become a mistress. Once again, Jane proves her integrity by not succumbing to Rochester's offers. Brontë has Jane Eyre holding onto her sense of self here; Jane is afraid that if she were to become a mistress, she would turn into someone Rochester couldn't respect.

Not wanting to be one of Rochester's possessions, she makes a great emotional sacrifice, and goes out into the world alone, again. She knows she is losing her greatest love, "her equal."

Jane sneaks out so she doesn't have to face Rochester again, and spends the night in emotional agony, yet "deliriously running" in the opposite direction of Millcote. She survives sleeping outdoors for two nights before her terror ends, somewhat, when a coachman picks her up.

Jane relies on God to get her through tough times, claiming it was God who gave her the energy to keep traveling. Jane prays when she spends the nights unsheltered, and says, "I felt the might and strength of God."

Study Questions

1. How is the wedding ceremony interrupted?

2. What is the relationship between Richard Mason and Bertha Rochester?

3. Where is the Mason family from?

4. How did Rochester come to marry Bertha?

5. How many years ago were they married?

6. What secret was kept from Rochester about the Mason family?

7. How does John Eyre figure in this chapter?

8. What is the solution Rochester offers to Jane?

9. What hastens Jane's retreat from Thornfield Hall?

10. How do we know this has been a devastating experience for Jane?

Answers

1. A lawyer, Mr. Briggs, reads a letter stating that Rochester had already been married.

2. They are sister and brother.

3. The Mason family is from the West Indies.

4. The marriage was arranged by his father.

5. They were married fifteen years ago.

6. There was a secret history of madness and insanity in the family.

7. It was a letter from John Eyre to Richard Mason that prompted Richard's appearance at the wedding.

8. Rochester first suggests she be his mistress, and then suggests they marry and move to the south of France.

9. Jane has a dream where she hears her mother telling her to flee.

10. Jane's description of her tremendous struggle with her decision, and her description of how painful it will be for her to leave Rochester is evidence of her devastation.

Suggested Essay Topics

1. Analyze Rochester's reasoning behind trying to marry Jane, when he is already married.

2. Describe how Jane's reaction and choice regarding Mr. Rochester's proposal are consistent with her character.

3. Discuss how Jane's dreams are prophetic.

Chapters XXVIII-XXIX

New Characters:

Diana and Mary Rivers: *sisters of St. John Rivers*

St. John Rivers: *minister of the parish at Morton, master of Moor House*

Hannah: *servant at Moor House*

Summary

Jane travels two days before she finally winds up at a crossroads and continues into a little town, called Morton. She discovers that she has left her money in the coach, so she is quite penniless. She wanders about the village, and goes into a store to ask for bread, but she becomes so embarrassed, she only asks to sit down.

She then goes around asking people if anyone needs a servant, but she receives negative responses from everyone. She continues to search for help; stopping at the parish church, where she is told by an old woman that the minister is away. She does not tell the old woman her predicament.

Jane is so hungry, she goes back, again, to the bread shop; thinking she will offer her handkerchief or gloves for payment, but the woman refuses, saying, "No, what could she do with them." Jane is disgusted with the whole process of begging. Toward evening, she walks past a farmer, and asks him for a piece of bread and he gives it to her.

It is getting near night and she sees a light off in the distance. She follows this light until she reaches the house, and looks through the kitchen window, observing a housekeeper and two young ladies.

Jane describes the scene. "A group of more interest appeared near the hearth, sitting still amidst the rosy peace and warmth suffusing it. Two young, graceful women–ladies in every point–sat, one in a low rocking-chair, the other on a lower stool; both wore deep mourning of crape and bombazine, which somber garb singularly set off very fair necks and faces; a large old pointer dog rested its massive head on the knee of one girl; in the lap of the other was cushioned a black cat."

Jane stands watching them a while, then after the girls go into another room, she remembers why she's there and knocks on the door. When the housekeeper, Hannah, opens the door, Jane asks if she can speak to the mistresses of the house, but the housekeeper will not call them and will not let her in. Jane, near death, just crumbles.

St. John arrives home just in time to hear Jane say, "I can but die, and I believe in God. Let me try to wait His will in silence." St. John responds with, "All men must die, but all are not condemned to meet a lingering and premature doom, such as yours would be if you perished here of want."

The family invites Jane in; they sit her by the fire, and Diana holds bread and milk to her mouth. "Try to eat," Diana says, and Mary repeats gently, "Yes try," while gently removing Jane's bonnet.

They ask Jane where she's from, but Jane is too tired to talk. When asked what her name is, Jane gives an alias, Jane Elliot.

St. John Rivers, Mary, and Diana retreat to another room to discuss her, and then return to assure Jane she can stay for the night. Hannah helps her to a small room where she sleeps in single bed.

It takes Jane four days in bed to recuperate from her ordeal. All the while she observes the Rivers family closely, listening to their conversations when they come into the room.

She hears the sisters say, "She is not an uneducated person, I should think, by her manner of speaking–her accent was quite pure; and the clothes she took off, though splashed and wet, were little worn and fine. She has a peculiar face; fleshless and haggard as it is, I rather like it; and when in good health and animated, I can fancy her physiognomy would be agreeable."

When St. John enters the room, he remarks to his sisters, "She looks sensible, but not at all handsome. Ill or well, she would always be plain. The grace and harmony of beauty are quite wanting in those features."

Diana responds, "Far otherwise. To speak truth, St. John, my heart rather warms to the poor little soul. I wish we may be able to benefit her permanently."

Jane is comforted by the warmth and affection she receives from Diana and Mary Rivers.

On the fourth day, she comes down and has a long conversation with the housekeeper, Hannah. Jane will not be put down by Hannah calling her a beggar. "You are mistaken in supposing me a beggar. I am no beggar, any more than yourself or your young ladies."

Jane learns through her conversation with Hannah that St. John is a minister, that Diana and Mary are his sisters, and that their father died only three weeks ago. The house they live in is called "Marsh End," or "Moor House."

Jane tells Hannah, rather severely, "You wished to turn me from the door, on a night when you should not have shut out a dog." When Hannah tells Jane not to think too badly of her, Jane responds, "But I do think hardly of you, and I'll tell you why–not so much because you refused to give me shelter, or regarded me as an impostor, as because you just now made it a species of reproach that I had no "brass" and no house. Some of the best people that ever lived have been as destitute as I am; and if you are a Christian, you ought not to consider poverty a crime."

Jane and Hannah eventually settle their differences, and shake hands.

The sisters arrive and suggest that Jane sit in the parlor, not the kitchen, and have some tea. St. John questions Jane about her past, but she says she can't discuss it now, and admits that her name is an alias, but still doesn't tell them her real name.

Jane asks if she might stay with them until she is able to find employment, and asks for St. John's help in finding a position. They question her about her marital status, and she blushes and tells them she is not married.

Analysis

Jane's stamina is tested, and once again, she relies on God. Her last words before going to sleep in a bed for the first time in three days are, "I thanked God."

In these chapters, Brontë addresses the issues of homelessness and poverty.

Jane, desperate, starving, without a penny and near death, is turned away by everyone she asks for help, except the Rivers family. She describes this as the "most terrible of situations, Reader it is not pleasant to dwell on these details. Some say there is enjoyment in looking back to painful experience past, but at this day I can scarcely bear to review the times to which I allude; the moral degradation, blent with the physical suffering, form too distressing a recollection ever to be willingly dwelt on."

Jane's conversation with Hannah also demonstrates her understanding of being homeless and poor, when she says, "Some of the best people who ever lived have been as destitute as I am."

The Rivers family has literally saved Jane's life. They represent the haven Jane sought in her wanderings. The scene in the kitchen, when Jane first looks upon Diana and Mary sitting in front of the hearth, is one of domestic bliss and contentment. The light in the window that led Jane to the house symbolizes the light of God, leading her to a better place. Jane has found comfort at last.

Jane's need to care for herself and be independent is again emphasized in these chapters. She immediately tells St. John after she recuperates, "I will be a dressmaker; I will be a plain workwoman; I will be a servant, a nurse-girl, if I can be no better."

She is willing to do anything to support herself, and asks if she can stay with the family until she finds a place. "I dread another essay of the horrors of homeless destitution." St. John responds by telling Jane, "If such is your spirit, I promise to aid you, in my own time and way." There have been people in this story who were cruel and pious, but these people are generous of spirit and action.

Study Questions

1. What is the name of the house where the Rivers family lives?

2. What happened to Jane when she first came to town?

3. How did Hannah react to Jane?

4. Was Moor House similar to Thornfield Hall?

5. How did the Rivers family decide to let Jane stay?

6. What did they surmise about Jane's background?

7. Why does Jane choose an alias?

8. What are the occupations of St. John Rivers, and his sisters, Diana and Mary?

9. How does St. John Rivers describe Jane?

10. What are Jane's observations of St. John Rivers?

Answers

1. The Rivers family lives at Marsh End, or Moor House.

2. She begs for food and money, but is not offered any help.

3. Hannah leaves her outside in the rain.

4. No, Moor House is a modest house, with small rooms, and homey but simple furnishings.

5. After observing her, they retreat to another room to discuss her in private, then return and bring her to bed.

6. They think she dresses well, and is educated because of the way she speaks.

7. She doesn't want to explain about her experience at Thornfield Hall.

8. St. John is a minister, and Diana and Mary are governesses.

9. He refers to her as a "half-frozen bird," and "not at all handsome."

10. She describes him as being handsome, but bland in personality.

Suggested Essay Topics

1. Describe Jane's experience as a beggar, and discuss how Jane's faith in God gives her the strength to survive.

2. Describe the characteristics of Diana, Mary, and St. John.

3. Analyze the symbolism of the light Jane follows to Moor House.

Chapters XXX – XXXI

New Characters:

Miss Rosamond Oliver: *admires St. John Rivers, daughter of Mr. Oliver*

Mr. Oliver: *father of Rosamond*

Summary

After a few days, Jane is well enough to be up and about. Jane finds she has a lot in common with Diana and Mary Rivers. They like to read, and are well educated, and enjoy sharing their knowledge with Jane.

Jane is particularly fond of Diana, who she describes as "superior and a leader." Diana offers to teach Jane German, and Jane thinks she is an excellent instructor. Jane, in turn, surprises and charms the sisters by giving them art lessons.

St. John Rivers is more remote, and doesn't spend that much time at home. When he is home, Jane thinks he is reserved and brooding. After hearing him preach, Jane describes his sermon. "Throughout; there was a strange bitterness; an absence of consolatory gentleness; stern allusions to Calvinistic doctrines–election, predestination, reprobation–were frequent; and each reference to these points sounded like a sentence pronounced for doom." Jane concludes that St. John is really not happy, and had not yet found "the peace of God."

A month passes, and it is time for Diana and Mary to leave Moor House for governess jobs with wealthy families in the south of England. Jane asks St. John whether he has found her a position, and he admits to finding nothing other than what he has to offer her; St. John's plan is to open a school for poor and orphaned girls.

He offers Jane the job of teacher (mistress of the school), and says that there is a cottage on the grounds of the school in which she can live. He explains that it is very modest, but comfortable. Miss Oliver, the daughter of the only rich man in Morton, had decorated the cottage, and also pays for the education and clothing for the orphans.

Jane accepts the job immediately. "In truth it was humble–but then, it was sheltered, and I wanted a safe asylum: it was plodding–but then, compared with that of a governess in a rich house, it was independent; and the fear of servitude with strangers entered my soul like iron: it was not ignoble–not unworthy–not mentally degrading. I made my decision." Jane is happy to become a teacher instead of a governess, and to be independent.

Diana and Mary are feeling sad about leaving their brother. Mary says, "we are now without father; we shall soon be without home and brother."

Bad news comes in the form of a letter: the Rivers' learn that their Uncle John is dead. Diana explains to Jane that he was their mother's brother, and had quarreled with their father many years ago. He had no other relatives besides them and "one other person."

It seems he has left all of his money to this other person and has left them only thirty guineas. Mary and Diana comment that they are a little disappointed that they will not be rich and that, "to John such a sum would have been valuable, for the good it would have enabled him to do."

Jane's cottage or "my home, then–when I at last find a home," is small but clean and adequate. Her job as a teacher is more challenging, since she is dealing with many children who are ignorant and coarse. Jane reminds herself, "I must not forget that these coarsely-clad little peasants are of flesh and blood as good as the scions of gentlest genealogy."

In spite of her new home and position Jane is still feeling depressed and lonely. She debates her choice of leaving Rochester. "Which is better?–To have surrendered to temptation, listened to passion; made no painful effort–no struggle." She concludes that she has made the right choice, "when I adhered to principle and law, and scorned and crushed the insane promptings of a frenzied moment."

Her thoughts result in her crying, and at that moment St. John comes in. He has brought some art supplies that Diana and Mary left for her. St. John, curious as to why she is upset, compares her experience to his, telling Jane how he had wanted to have a literary life before he entered the ministry, but he responded to God's call. He suggests she "resist every temptation to look back."

While they are talking, Miss Oliver comes in. Jane describes her as a "perfect beauty." She tells the reader how St. John, flushed, "looked nearly as beautiful for a man as she for a woman."

Although Miss Oliver practically begs St. John to come and visit her father, St. John is adamant about not going. "Not tonight, Miss Rosamond, not tonight."

Miss Oliver tells Jane she will visit her at the school.

Analysis

Jane has found the Rivers sisters to be similar to her in style and education, and they bond with her as well. Brontë's description of her relationship with the Rivers sisters reflects her own close, happy relationship with her dear sisters, Emily and Anne.

St. John is another story. Although a minister, Jane finds him cold, and lacking in passion. He does not find satisfaction in his Christian duties; he just goes through the motions.

Jane's sense of self, and need for independence is brought out again. In her reasoning for accepting the job as a teacher she mentions, "it was independent." Again, the feelings Brontë describes in Jane mirror her own experiences when she worked briefly as a teacher.

Similarly, in exploring her feelings for Rochester, she comes to the conclusion that she made the right choice in leaving him instead of being his mistress. Although she admits that "He did love me–no one will ever love me so again," to Jane it is more important to be "free and honest," then to "be a slave in a fool's paradise at Marseilles."

A mysterious element is introduced in this chapter. The Rivers family has been left an inheritance from their "Uncle John," but he has given the bulk of his money to another unknown relative.

When Miss Oliver appears, Jane recognizes St. John's attraction for her. "I saw a glow rise to the master's face."

Study Questions

1. What do the Rivers sisters have in common with Jane?
2. Why does Jane admire Diana?
3. What is Jane's observation of St. John?
4. What, and where, is Jane's new home?
5. Who are her pupils?
6. Who dies and leaves the Rivers family a small inheritance?
7. How does Jane describe Miss Oliver?
8. What is Miss Oliver's connection to the school?
9. Who is Mr. Oliver?
10. How does St. John react to Miss Oliver?

Answers

1. They all love reading, and are well educated.
2. She admires her strength and leadership qualities.
3. She thinks him cold, and lacking in passion.

4. Jane's new home is a cottage on the grounds of the school.

5. Jane's pupils are mostly poor, uneducated children of farmers.

6. Their "Uncle John" leaves the Rivers family a small inheritance upon his death.

7. Jane describes Miss Oliver as a "perfect beauty."

8. Miss Oliver is the benefactress of the school.

9. Mr. Oliver is Miss Oliver's father; the sole rich man in the town of Morton.

10. Jane observes him blushing in Miss Oliver's presence, and realizes that he is in love with Miss Oliver.

Suggested Essay Topics

1. Discuss why Jane believes the life of a teacher is better than that of a governess.

2. Characterize St. John Rivers.

3. Examine Jane's camaraderie with Diana and Mary Rivers.

4. Discuss the job options for a woman in the Victorian Age.

5. Explain Jane's new sense of achievement.

Chapters XXXII – XXXIII

Summary

Jane adjusts to her new lifestyle, eventually gaining the trust of the town people. "I felt I had become a favorite in the neighborhood. Whenever I went out, I heard on all sides cordial salutations, and was welcomed with friendly smiles." At night, Jane's mind is tormented by dreams about Rochester.

She describes how she would "rush into strange dreams at night: dreams many–colored, agitated, full of the ideal, the stirring, the stormy–dreams where, amidst unusual scenes charged with adventure, with agitating risk and romantic chance, I still again and again met Mr. Rochester, always at some exciting crisis; and then the sense of being in his arms, hearing his voice, meeting his eye, touching his hand, his cheek, loving him, being loved by him–the hope of passing a lifetime at his side, would be renewed, with all its force and fire."

Rosamond Oliver visits the school regularly and Jane observes how her presence would cause St. John's "cheek to glow." Jane grows fond of Miss Oliver, whom she describes as coquettish, but not heartless; exacting, but not worthlessly selfish." Miss Oliver asks Jane to draw a portrait of her, and Jane is delighted "at the idea of copying from so perfect and radiant a model."

Mr. Oliver becomes impressed by his daughter's portrait and invites Jane to their home. During Jane's conversation with Mr. Oliver, she discovers that he is fond of St. John, and would not oppose a match with his daughter. Mr. Oliver thought "it a pity that so fine and talented a man should have formed the design of going out as a missionary; it was quite throwing a valuable life away."

When Jane speaks with St. John next, she tells him that Miss Oliver does indeed like him and Rivers admits to loving Rosamond Oliver, but that, "I experience at the same time a calm, unwarped consciousness that she would not make me a good wife; that she is not the partner suited to me."

Jane goes on to tell him he does not have to be a missionary, if Rosamond would not make a missionary's wife, but he exclaims, "Relinquish! What! my vocation? My great work? My foundation laid on earth for a mansion in heaven."

When he leaves the room, St. John suddenly tears off a piece of paper that Jane is using to lean on. Jane dismisses the moment as unimportant.

The next day a snowstorm covers the valley. Jane is reading, when she is surprised by St. John who comes in, "white as a glacier." St. John is so excited that Jane thinks "his wits were touched. If he were insane, however, his was a very cool and collected insanity." After a while St. John narrates a story to her about a "poor curate–never mind his name at this moment–fell in love with a rich man's daughter."

He obviously is describing Jane's life, and she listens until he gets to Mr. Rochester. She then interrupts, and wants to know what St. John knows of Mr. Rochester, but he says "nothing."

He continues his story. It seems that when he snatched Jane's paper it had the signature Jane Eyre on it, and a Mr. Briggs, John Eyre's solicitor, has been looking for a Jane Eyre because she has been left an inheritance by her uncle.

St. John then explains how they are related. "My mother's name was Eyre; she had two brothers: one a clergyman, who married Miss Jane Reed of Gateshead; the other, John Eyre, Esq., merchant, late of Funchal, Madeira." Jane is extremely happy to have three new relations.

Jane is saddened to know of her uncle's death, and shocked by the large sum of money she will be receiving. But her real delight is in knowing she is related to the Rivers family. "Oh, I am glad!–I am glad," Jane exclaims. At first, St. John thinks it is the money she is talking about, and is shocked when he realizes it is her new found family that Jane is thrilled about. "You, cannot at all imagine the craving I have for fraternal and sisterly love. I never had a home, I never had brothers or sisters; I must and will have them now," she says. Jane describes her plan to divide the 20,000 pounds with her newfound relatives.

St. John tries to convince Jane to keep all of the inheritance for herself, but Jane is adamant about sharing it. She sees a chance to repay the Rivers' for saving her life, and decides that she will share all of her inheritance equally with St. John, Diana, and Mary. It is also decided that she will stay on at the school until St. John finds another teacher. St. John suggests that perhaps she will marry someday, but Jane says, "Nonsense again! Marry! I don't want to marry, and I never shall marry."

Analysis

Jane gains respect and independence in her new lifestyle. "To live amidst general regard, though it be but the regard of working people," is like "sitting in sunshine, calm and sweet." She has obviously grown into a woman with confidence, but she also reveals some of the same snobbery that has blighted her life.

Her passion and love for Rochester, however, are still expressed in her dreams. She awakes from her dreams, "trembling and quivering; and then the still, dark night witnessed the convulsion of despair, and heard the burst of passion."

Jane exposes St. John as a hypocrite; willing to deny his true feelings for Rosamond Oliver to pursue the ministry. Jane's description of St. John's reaction to Rosamond details his predicament. "In spite of his Christian stoicism, when she went up and addressed him, and smiled gaily, encouragingly, even fondly in his face, his hand would tremble and his eye burn. He seemed to say, with his sad and resolute look, if he did not say it with his lips, 'I love you, and I know you prefer me. It is not despair of success that keeps me dumb. If I offered my heart, I believe you would accept it. But the heart is already laid on a sacred altar; the fire is arranged around it. It will soon be no more than a sacrifice consumed.' "

Jane shocks St. John by explicitly detailing his reactions to Miss Oliver, to which St. John says, "you are original." Jane considers St. John's denying his love for Rosamond to be very strange.

Chapter XXXII ends with a mysterious element added: St. John apparently saw something on Jane's papers that made him tear a piece off.

The mystery is explained in the next chapter when Jane learns of her inheritance and new relations. Jane sees a chance to repay the Rivers for saving her life, and it brings her joy to be able to give them the financial security of 5,000 pounds each.

Jane plans to live at Moor House. "I am resolved I will have a home and connections. I like Moor House, and I will live at Moor House; I like Diana and Mary, and I will attach myself for life to Diana and Mary."

It is quite a coincidence, another device used by Brontë, that the people who saved her life also wind up being her only living relatives, and that she is suddenly an heiress whose generosity can make her relatives financially secure.

Study Questions

1. How has Jane's status changed?

2. What does she observe about St. John Rivers and Rosamond Oliver?

3. What does Mr. Oliver tell Jane?

4. How are Jane's dreams different from her days?

5. Why does Miss Oliver like Jane?

6. How does Jane shock St. John?

7. What language is Jane studying?

8. How does St. John feel about Rosamond Oliver?

9. What does St. John do with Jane's paper?

10. What is Jane's reaction to St. John's attention to her paper?

Answers

1. She is now regarded with respect by the towns-people.

2. St. John and Miss Oliver are attracted to each other.

3. Mr. Oliver tells Jane that he would not oppose a match between his daughter and St. John.

4. Her days are quiet and orderly, and her dreams are excited and passionate.

5. Miss Oliver respects Jane's mind and talent.

6. Jane shocks St. John by telling him, "you tremble and become flushed when ever Miss Oliver enters the school-room."

7. Jane is studying German.

8. He loves her, but does not think she is suited to missionary life.

9. He tears off a piece of a paper she is leaning on while painting.

10. She dismisses it as unimportant.

Suggested Essay Topics

1. Characterize Rosamond Oliver.

2. Discuss Jane's new status and sense of accomplishment.

3. Explain Jane's decision to share her inheritance.

4. Examine St. John's ambition to be a minister.

Chapters XXXIV – XXXV

Summary

Christmas is approaching and the Morton School is closed. Jane returns to Moor House with Hannah to await the arrival of Diana and Mary. Jane redecorates and cleans the house. Diana and Mary are delighted with the changes she has made, but St. John remains as cool as always.

The women spend a happy week together. One night as St. John is saying goodnight to everyone, he kisses Diana and Mary, but not Jane. Diana pushes Jane towards him, and tells St. John to treat Jane as his sister, also.

Jane describes St. John's kiss. "There are no such things as marble kisses, or ice kisses, or I should say my ecclesiastical cousin's salute belonged to one of these classes; but there may be experiment kisses, and his was an experiment kiss."

Meanwhile, St. John asks Jane to help him study Hindostanee; he will be leaving for India in three weeks. Since it will only be for three months, Jane agrees.

Jane reminds the reader that she has not forgotten Mr. Rochester, that every night she goes to her room, "to brood over it." She writes a letter to Mrs. Fairfax trying to find out information, but she receives no reply.

One day, St. John asks Jane to go for a walk in the Marsh Glen. He asks Jane to come with him overseas, and be a missionary's wife. Jane responds, "I do not understand a missionary life: I have never studied missionary labors."

St. John tries to convince her by describing her attributes for this position. "Jane, you are docile, diligent, disinterested, faithful, constant, and courageous; very gentle, and very heroic: cease to mistrust yourself–I can trust you unreservedly. As a conductor of Indian schools, and a helper amongst Indian women, your assistance will be invaluable."

Jane cannot consider the idea of being his wife, but comes up with another plan: "I am ready to go to India, if I may go free," she says. He argues that she must go as his wife, and Jane responds by telling him to "seek one elsewhere than in me, St. John; seek one fitted to you."

He continues to argue his point, stating that he could never travel alone with a girl of nineteen, until Jane finally gets through to him by saying, "I scorn your idea of love....I scorn the counterfeit sentiment you offer: yes, St. John, and I scorn you when you offer it."

That night St. John kisses Diana and Mary goodnight, but doesn't even shake hands with Jane. Jane goes after him, at Diana's suggestion, to make amends. Jane asks for his handshake and finds it a "cold, loose touch he impressed on my fingers!"

Before St. John leaves, Jane tries to make amends with him, again, and again he asks, "and you will not marry me." Jane describes his demeanor, "reader, do you know, as I do, what terror those cold people can put into the ice of their questions? How much of the fall of the avalanche is in their anger? – of the breaking up of the frozen sea in their displeasure." Jane still replies, "No St. John, I will not marry you. I adhere to my resolution."

St. John wants to know if she is going to look for Rochester, and when Jane admits, "I must find out what is become of him," St. John tell her, "It remains for me then, to remember you in my prayers; and to entreat God for you, in all earnestness, that you may not indeed become a castaway. I had thought I recognized in you one of the chosen. But God sees not as man sees: His will be done."

The night before St. John leaves, Jane goes to him to seek his friendship. St. John asks her to reconsider. "He pressed his hand firmer on my head, as if he claimed me: he surrounded me with his arm, almost as if he loved me (I say almost–I knew the difference–for I had felt what it was to be loved; but, like him, I had now put love out of the question, and thought only of duty.)"

Jane is softening up to St. John when she describes; "the flesh quivering on my bones," after she hears Rochester's unmistakable voice calling, "Jane, Jane! Jane!"

She runs off to her room, "and prayed in my way–a different way to St. John's, but effective in its own fashion."

Analysis

Jane reassures the reader she is still thinking about Mr. Rochester, her one true love. In contrast, St. John, although zealous in his religious convictions, is cold and unfeeling. His proposal to Jane is one of convenience, and Jane cannot settle for living a life that is a lie. She analyzes his proposal and comes to the conclusion that, "If I join St. John, I abandon half myself: if I go to India, I go to premature death."

Here again, we can see how Rochester and Jane share the same sense of integrity. Just as Rochester could not marry Blanche Ingram, although they were socially matched, because he did not love her; Jane cannot marry St. John Rivers because she does not love him.

St. John almost breaks Jane down with his sermons and pressure. "The impossible–that is, my marriage with St. John–was fast becoming the Possible. All was changing utterly with a sudden sweep. Religion called–angels beckoned–God commanded." But before she actually consents to the marriage, Jane hears Rochester calling her name.

Study Questions

1. What time of year is it?
2. How did Jane prepare Moor House for Diana's and Mary's return?
3. Why does St. John want to marry Jane?
4. Why does she refuse him?
5. What did Diana think of this idea?
6. How does Jane constantly describe St. John?
7. What happened to Rosamond Oliver?
8. What does Jane say when St. John asks her if she will look for Mr. Rochester?
9. What stops Jane from giving in to St. John's request?
10. What does Jane say when she hears Rochester calling her name?

Answers

1. It is Christmas time.

2. Jane cleaned and redecorated the house.

3. He thinks Jane would make a good missionary wife.

4. She knows he doesn't love her, and she doesn't love him.

5. Diana agreed with Jane, that missionary life would not be for her, but she says that St. John is a good man.

6. St. John is described as extremely cold and unfeeling.

7. Miss Oliver married someone else.

8. Jane tells St. John she must find out what happened to Rochester.

9. She hears Rochester call her name.

10. "I am coming, wait for me! Oh, I will come."

Suggested Essay Topics

1. Compare St. John Rivers with Mr. Rochester.

2. Discuss Jane's reasoning in rejecting St. John's proposal.

3. Discuss St. John's reasoning in rejecting Rosamond Oliver for a wife, and pursuing Jane.

Chapters XXXVI – XXXVIII

New Character:

The Host: *former butler of Edward Rochester's father, and the innkeeper of the Rochester Arms*

Summary

The next day, Jane stays in her room until St. John leaves. He slips a note under her door, asking for her decision, but doesn't talk to her. At breakfast, Jane tells Diana and Mary that she is going on a journey for four days "to see or hear news of a friend about whom I had for some time been uneasy."

When Jane reaches Thornfield she is shocked to see "a blackened ruin." Jane goes to the Rochester Arms Inn, and asks The Host if he has any information. The Host details the circumstances of the fire that left Thornfield Hall in ruins: it seems that Mrs. Poole had been drinking, so Bertha Rochester, unattended, started the fire in the governess' bed.

He explains to Jane how the servants knew of Rochester's love for the governess, and his desolation when she ran off. Continuing with the fire story, The Host tells how Rochester helped all of the servants out of the house, and then tried to save Bertha, but she was on the roof, and jumped to her death.

A beam fell on Rochester when he was leaving the house, and he was left blind, and one of his hands had to be amputated. He tells Jane that Rochester now resides at Ferndean, his manor house, approximately thirty miles away.

Jane takes a carriage directly to Ferndean. At first she observes Rochester from outside the house as he comes out for a walk. Then she goes inside and tells John and Mary that she would like to see Mr. Rochester. They say he won't see anyone, but when he rings the parlor bell, Jane takes in his water on a tray.

Rochester greets Jane with great passion. "In truth?–in the flesh? My living Jane?...My living darling!" Jane tells him she will never leave him again, and kisses his injured eye.

Jane goes on to tell him that she is rich. "I am an independent woman now."

He wants to know all about her experiences, but she says she is too tired to talk about it, it is too late. He suggest she might think him ugly. "Am I hideous, Jane?" Jane replies, "Very sir; you always were, you know."

She tells him she has been with "good people." He wants to know about them. "Whom the deuce have you been with?...Whom have you been with Jane?" She tells him he will have to wait for the morning.

They spend the next morning outdoors. Jane describes to Rochester how "the flowers and hedges looked refreshed; how sparkling blue the sky." Jane seats him on "a dry stump of a tree," and sits on his knee.

Rochester is anxious to hear her tale. "What could my darling do, left destitute and penniless? And what did she do? Let me hear now."

Jane begins her story, glossing over the three days she nearly starved to death. Rochester says she should have confided in him, that he would never have forced her to be his mistress. She says her sufferings were short, and they led her to obtain "the office of school mistress, etc. The accession of fortune, the discovery of my relations."

Rochester questions Jane; she endures his "cross-examination" about St. John. When he hears that St. John asked Jane to marry him, he accuses her of lying. When she indignantly convinces him otherwise, he wants to know why she sits on his knee if she loves another.

Jane describes St. John's love: "He does not love me; I do not love him. He loves (as he can love, and that is not as you love) a beautiful young lady called Rosamond." After Jane convinces Rochester of her love, he expresses another worry. "I am no better than the old lightning-struck chestnut tree in Thornfield orchard." Jane assures him of her love and accepts his proposal.

Rochester exclaims his joy, and tells Jane, "you think me, I dare say, an irreligious dog; but my heart swells with gratitude to the beneficent God of this earth just now." He goes on to tell her how four days ago, between eleven and twelve o'clock, he was feeling so desolate, he prayed to God, and called out Jane's name, "Jane! Jane! Jane!"

The most amazing part was what he heard, "a voice it was, replied, 'I am coming: Wait for me'; and a moment after, went whispering on the wind the words, 'Where are you?'"

Jane feels she cannot speak about her experience, but comments to the Reader, "The coincidence struck me as too awful and inexplicable to be communicated."

Rochester thanks God, again, for his good fortune, and Jane describes their walk toward the house. "Then he stretched his hand out to be led, I took that dear hand, held it a moment to my lips, then let it pass round my shoulder; being so much lower of stature than he, I served both for his prop and guide. We entered the wood, and wended homeward."

In Chapter XXXVIII (conclusion), Jane begins, "Reader, I married him." Jane tells the servants, John and Mary, who are happy for her; and writes to Diana and Mary Rivers telling them of her marriage also. They are pleased and supportive.

St. John writes to Jane but never mentions Rochester's name, so she's not sure if he knows she's married or not. When he writes, St. John says to Jane: "he hopes I am happy, and trusts I am not of those who live without God in the world, and only mind earthly things."

Jane brings the reader up-to-date about Adele. Jane brings her home from a harsh boarding school, at first thinking she will be her governess again, but then realizes, "my time and cares were now required by another–my husband needed them all."

Adele goes to a school nearby where they can visit her often. Jane tells us that Adele grows into a good companion, and that, "a sound English education corrected in a great measure her French defects." Jane closes the novel by saying, "I have now been married ten years." She is very happy with her life. They have a son, and Rochester has regained partial sight.

Diana and Mary have married, and visit her once year. St. John remains in India, unmarried, and Jane believes that soon he will be "called at length into the joy of his Lord."

Analysis

Brontë takes Jane on a great emotional search to prove the theme of retribution or that "good comes to good." Both Jane and Rochester go through enormous suffering, yet each, in the end, find happiness because of their basic good souls.

Although Rochester did deceive Jane by trying to take her for his wife when he already had one, he does suffer for his sins. In the end, his goodness prevailed in the face of danger. The Host tells Jane, "it was all his own courage, and a body may say, his kindness, in a way, ma'am: he wouldn't leave the house till everyone else was out before him."

Jane teases Rochester along for a while about her relationship with St. John, but then she has to admit that he does not love in the same way as Rochester. Jane recognizes that although St. John thinks of himself as a disciple, his sacrifices and energies are not lightened by warmth.

Brontë's belief in mystical forces is again portrayed in these chapters, as Jane and Rochester's love is saved by the mysterious voices in the night. Jane thinks it so extraordinary that she decides not to tell Rochester about it. Rochester thanks God for this miracle. Jane and Rochester belong together because they are emotional and intellectual equals.

In the conclusion, Jane marries and cares for Rochester, yet still reaffirms her independence and her new sense of security. She doesn't have to worry about being consumed or swallowed up by him, because now she has self–confidence, and her own money. Jane has proven to herself that she can stand on her own.

Although the ending of the novel typifies the Victorian romantic fantasy (happiness for a woman meant marriage to a rich man), Jane returns to Rochester in total control of the situation.

Jane has a strong sense of who she is, and knows that she can function independently. She is proud of her achievements: she was a teacher, she found a loving family, and most importantly she was financially independent. "I told you I am independent, sir, as well as rich; I am my own mistress."

Although it is a theme of the book that virtue can be present in the absence of money and that money doesn't guarantee virtue, Jane's happy ending includes wealth.

As Jane and Rochester walk toward the house, she is considerably smaller then he, yet he again leans on her. They are actually "equals," in strength of character, passion, and intellect.

Study Questions

1. Why does Jane go to look for Rochester?

2. What stops her, at the last minute, from giving in to St. John?

3. How does Diana react to knowing that Jane turned down St. John's proposal?

4. How does Jane find Thornfield Hall?

5. Where does she stay?

6. What does The Host tell Jane?

7. What is Rochester's reaction to having Jane come back to him?

8. What mystical occurrence does Rochester describe?

9. How has Rochester's philosophy changed?

10. What becomes of Diana, Mary, and St. John Rivers?

Answers

1. She can't stop thinking or dreaming about him.

2. She hears Rochester's voice calling her name.

3. Diana supports Jane, recognizing St. John's faults, but calling him a "good man."

4. Thornfield Hall is burned to the ground.

5. Jane stays at the Rochester Arms Inn, where The Host informs her of Rochester's fate.

6. Rochester is blind and maimed; Bertha has died in the fire she started.

7. He cannot be more passionate about his feelings. He reacts jealousy to St. John and is worried that Jane will not love his deformed body.

8. He called out for Jane in the middle of the night, and he heard "a voice" answer him.

9. Rochester has a new faith in God, and openly prays.

10. Diana marries a sea-captain, Mary marries a clergyman, and they visit every year. St. John stays in India, and Jane fears he will be with God soon.

Suggested Essay Topics

1. Discuss the attributes that make Jane and Rochester equals.

2. Examine some of the symbols contributing to the richness of the scene with Rochester and Jane reunited.

3. Examine the mystical experience both Jane and Rochester have.

4. Discuss the terms in which Jane marries Rochester.
5. Explain Jane's/Brontë's view of Christian love.

Sample Analytical Paper Topics

Topic #1

Choose one or more aspects of Charlotte Brontë's life and discuss how she transferred these facts into fiction in *Jane Eyre.*

Outline

I. Thesis Statement: *Many aspects and experiences of Charlotte Brontë's life can be seen in Jane Eyre's life.*

    A. Background of Victorian England

        1. Views on child rearing

        2. Roles for woman

II. Charlotte Brontë's Early Life

    A. Daughters of the Clergy School at Cowan Bridge

        1. Harsh treatment

        2. Death of sisters Maria and Elizabeth

    B. Lowood School

        1. Harsh treatment

        2. Death of Helen Burns

III. Education

    A. Charlotte's work as a teacher and governess

       1.   Roe Head

   B.   Jane's work as a teacher and governess

       1.   Thornfield Hall

IV. Romantic hero

   A.   Charlotte and Constantin Heger

   B.   Jane and Rochester

Topic #2

Examine Charlotte Brontë's religious background, and how she presented her Christian values through the novel *Jane Eyre*.

Outline

I.   Thesis Statement: *Charlotte Brontë's religious beliefs and Christian values were represented by a variety of characters in the novel* Jane Eyre.

II.   Introduction

   A.   Religion in Victorian England

   B.   Charlotte Brontë's religious background

       1.   Her parents

       2.   Her education

III. Characters

   A.   As seen through Jane's eyes

       1.   Mrs. Reed

       2.   Mr. Brocklehurst

       3.   St. John Rivers

       4.   Helen Burns

       5.   Miss Temple

       6.   Mr. Rochester

   B.   Jane's Christian values for herself

       1.   Her moral beliefs

2. Her integrity

3. Her reliance on God to give her strength

Topic #3

Jane's sense of self is evident from the very first time we meet her. Discuss her independent actions.

Outline

I.   Thesis Statement: *Throughout her life, Jane Eyre makes a determined effort to adhere to her strong sense of self and independence.*

II. Early life

    A.   Gateshead Hall

        1.   The Red Room

        2.   Her verbal attacks at Mrs. Reed

        3.   Her honesty to Mr. Brocklehurst

    B.   Lowood School

        1.   Her stamina to keep going against all adversity

        2.   Her striving for education

        3.   Her need to take care of herself

    C.   Thornfield Hall

        1.   Her brutal honesty with Rochester

        2.   Her flee from temptation

    D.   Morton

        1.   Establishing herself as a teacher

        2.   Reacting to St. John's proposal

        3.   Receiving an inheritance

    E.   Ferndean

        1.   Returning to Rochester on her own terms

2.   Achieving independence through money and education

3.   Knowledge of self

Topic #4

Discuss Jane's search for love, and the various relationships in which she finds love.

Outline

I.   Thesis Statement: *Jane Eyre, being an orphan raised by a cruel relation, desperately needs love and companionship, which she does find in various relationships throughout her life.*

II.   Gateshead Hall

    A.   Bessie

III. Lowood School

    A.   Miss Temple

    B.   Helen Burns

IV.   Thornfield Hall

    A.   Adele

    B.   Mr. Rochester

V.   Moor House

    A.   Diana and Mary

VI.   Her final relationship and marriage to Rochester.

Bibliography

Bentley, Phyllis. *The Brontës*. London: Thames and Hudson Ltd., 1969.

Blom, Margaret Howard. *Charlotte Brontë*. Boston: C.K. Hall & Co., 1977.

Brontë, Charlotte. *Jane Eyre*. New York: E. M. Hale & Company, 2nd edition.

Cecil, David. *Early Victorian Novelists*. New York: The Bobbs-Merrill Company, 1935.

Evans, Barbara and Gareth Lloyd. *The Scribner Companion to The Brontës*. New York: Charles Scribner's Sons, 1982.

Gaskell, Elizabeth Cleghorn. *The Life of Charlotte Brontë*. London: J.M. Dent, 1960. First published 1857.

Himmelfarb, Gertrude. *Victorian Minds*. New York: Alfred A. Knopf, Inc. 1968.

Laver, James. *Victorian Vista*. Boston: Houghton Mifflin Company, 1955.

Martin, Robert Bernard. *The Accents of Persuasion, Charlotte Brontë's Novels*. New York: W. W. Norton & Company, Inc., 1966.

Moglen, Helen. *Charlotte Brontë: The Self Conceived*. New York: W. W. Norton & Company, Inc., 1976.

Peters, Margot. *Unquiet Soul, A Biography of Charlotte Brontë*. New York: Doubleday & Company, Inc., 1975.

REA's Test Preps
The Best in Test Preparation

- REA "Test Preps" are **far more** comprehensive than any other test preparation series
- Each book contains up to **eight** full-length practice tests based on the most recent exam
- **Every** type of question likely to be given on the exams is included
- Answers are accompanied by **full** and **detailed** explanations

REA publishes over 60 Test Preparation volumes in several series. They include:

Advanced Placement Exams(APs)
Biology
Calculus AB & Calculus BC
Chemistry
Computer Science
Economics
English Language & Composition
English Literature & Composition
European History
Government & Politics
Physics B & C
Psychology
Spanish Language
Statistics
United States History

College-Level Examination Program (CLEP)
Analyzing and Interpreting Literature
College Algebra
Freshman College Composition
General Examinations
General Examinations Review
History of the United States I
History of the United States II
Human Growth and Development
Introductory Sociology
Principles of Marketing
Spanish

SAT II: Subject Tests
Biology E/M
Chemistry
English Language Proficiency Test
French
German

SAT II: Subject Tests (cont'd)
Literature
Mathematics Level IC, IIC
Physics
Spanish
United States History
Writing

Graduate Record Exams (GREs)
Biology
Chemistry
Computer Science
General
Literature in English
Mathematics
Physics
Psychology

ACT - ACT Assessment

ASVAB - Armed Services Vocational Aptitude Battery

CBEST - California Basic Educational Skills Test

CDL - Commercial Driver License Exam

CLAST - College Level Academic Skills Test

COOP & HSPT - Catholic High School Admission Tests

ELM - California State University Entry Level Mathematics Exam

FE (EIT) - Fundamentals of Engineering Exams - For both AM & PM Exams

FTCE - Florida Teacher Certification Exam

GED - High School Equivalency Diploma Exam (U.S. & Canadian editions)

GMAT CAT - Graduate Management Admission Test

LSAT - Law School Admission Test

MAT- Miller Analogies Test

MCAT - Medical College Admission Test

MTEL - Massachusetts Tests for Educator Licensure

MSAT- Multiple Subjects Assessment for Teachers

NJ HSPA - New Jersey High School Proficiency Assessment

NYSTCE: LAST & ATS-W - New York State Teacher Certification

PLT - Principles of Learning & Teaching Tests

PPST- Pre-Professional Skills Tests

PSAT - Preliminary Scholastic Assessment Test

SAT

TExES - Texas Examinations of Educator Standards

THEA - Texas Higher Education Assessment

TOEFL - Test of English as a Foreign Language

TOEIC - Test of English for International Communication

USMLE Steps 1,2,3 - U.S. Medical Licensing Exams

U.S. Postal Exams 460 & 470

RESEARCH & EDUCATION ASSOCIATION
61 Ethel Road W. • Piscataway, New Jersey 08854
Phone: (732) 819-8880   **website: www.rea.com**

Please send me more information about your Test Prep books

Name _____

Address _____

City _____ State _____ Zip _____

REA's
HANDBOOK OF
ENGLISH
Grammar, Style, and Writing

All the essentials you need to know are contained in this simple and practical book

Learn quickly and easily
- **Rules and exceptions in grammar**
- **Spelling and proper punctuation**
- **Common errors in sentence structure**
- **2,000 examples of correct usage**
- **Effective writing skills**

Complete practice exercises with answers follow each chapter

REA *Research & Education Association*

Available at your local bookstore or order directly from us by sending in coupon below.

RESEARCH & EDUCATION ASSOCIATION
61 Ethel Road W., Piscataway, New Jersey 08854
Phone: (732) 819-8880   website: www.rea.com

VISA   **MasterCard**

Charge Card Number

☐ Payment enclosed
☐ Visa ☐ MasterCard

Expiration Date: _____ / _____
                    Mo   Yr

Please ship **"Handbook of English"** @ $22.95 plus $4.00 for shipping.

Name _____

Address _____

City _____ State _____ Zip _____

REA's **Problem Solvers**

The "PROBLEM SOLVERS" are comprehensive supplemental text-books designed to save time in finding solutions to problems. Each "PROBLEM SOLVER" is the first of its kind ever produced in its field. It is the product of a massive effort to illustrate almost any imaginable problem in exceptional depth, detail, and clarity. Each problem is worked out in detail with a step-by-step solution, and the problems are arranged in order of complexity from elementary to advanced. Each book is fully indexed for locating problems rapidly.

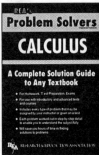

ACCOUNTING
ADVANCED CALCULUS
ALGEBRA & TRIGONOMETRY
AUTOMATIC CONTROL
  SYSTEMS/ROBOTICS
BIOLOGY
BUSINESS, ACCOUNTING, & FINANCE
CALCULUS
CHEMISTRY
COMPLEX VARIABLES
COMPUTER SCIENCE
DIFFERENTIAL EQUATIONS
ECONOMICS
ELECTRICAL MACHINES
ELECTRIC CIRCUITS
ELECTROMAGNETICS
ELECTRONIC COMMUNICATIONS
ELECTRONICS
FINITE & DISCRETE MATH
FLUID MECHANICS/DYNAMICS
GENETICS
GEOMETRY

HEAT TRANSFER
LINEAR ALGEBRA
MACHINE DESIGN
MATHEMATICS for ENGINEERS
MECHANICS
NUMERICAL ANALYSIS
OPERATIONS RESEARCH
OPTICS
ORGANIC CHEMISTRY
PHYSICAL CHEMISTRY
PHYSICS
PRE-CALCULUS
PROBABILITY
PSYCHOLOGY
STATISTICS
STRENGTH OF MATERIALS &
  MECHANICS OF SOLIDS
TECHNICAL DESIGN GRAPHICS
THERMODYNAMICS
TOPOLOGY
TRANSPORT PHENOMENA
VECTOR ANALYSIS

*If you would like more information about any of these books,
complete the coupon below and return it to us or visit your local bookstore.*

RESEARCH & EDUCATION ASSOCIATION
61 Ethel Road W. • Piscataway, New Jersey 08854
Phone: (908) 819-8880

Please send me more information about your Problem Solver Books

Name _____

Address _____

City _____ State _____ Zip _____

Available at your local bookstore or order directly from us by sending in coupon below.

RESEARCH & EDUCATION ASSOCIATION
61 Ethel Road W., Piscataway, New Jersey 08854
Phone: (732) 819-8880   website: www.rea.com

VISA   **MasterCard**

Charge Card Number

☐ Payment enclosed
☐ Visa ☐ MasterCard

Expiration Date: _____ / _____
                      Mo   Yr

Please ship REA's **"AP English Language & Composition"** @ $19.95 plus $4.00 for shipping.

Name _____

Address _____

City _____ State _____ Zip _____

Available at your local bookstore or order directly from us by sending in coupon below.

RESEARCH & EDUCATION ASSOCIATION
61 Ethel Road W., Piscataway, New Jersey 08854
Phone: (732) 819-8880   website: www.rea.com

VISA **MasterCard**

Charge Card Number

☐ Payment enclosed
☐ Visa   ☐ MasterCard

Expiration Date: _____ / _____
Mo   Yr

Please ship REA's **"ACT – Software Edition"** @ $29.95 plus $4.00 for shipping.

Name _____

Address _____

City _____ State _____ Zip _____